DECADES OF THE AIRLINERS

BRANIFF
TEXACO

DECADES OF THE AIRLINERS

The 1970s

GEORGE W. HAMLIN

FONTHILL

First published in Great Britain in 2026 by
Fonthill
An imprint of
Pen & Sword Books Ltd
Yorkshire – Philadelphia

ISBN 978-1-03619-266-2

A CIP catalogue record for this book
is available from the British Library.

Typeset in SabonLTStd 10/13 by
SJmagic DESIGN SERVICES, India.
Printed and bound in India by Replika Press Pvt Ltd

FSC
www.fsc.org
MIX
Paper | Supporting
responsible forestry
FSC™ C016779

The Publisher's authorised representative in the EU for product
safety is Authorised Rep Compliance Ltd., Ground Floor,
71 Lower Baggot Street, Dublin D02 P593, Ireland.
www.arccompliance.com

For a complete list of Pen & Sword titles please contact
PEN & SWORD BOOKS LIMITED
George House, Units 12 & 13, Beevor Street, Off Pontefract Road,
Barnsley, South Yorkshire, S71 1HN, England
E-mail: enquiries@pen-and-sword.co.uk
Website: www.pen-and-sword.co.uk

or

PEN AND SWORD BOOKS
1950 Lawrence Rd, Havertown, PA 19083, USA
E-mail: uspen-and-sword@casematepublishers.com
Website: www.penandswordbooks.com

To Noel Schachner, who was there when a number of the early photos were taken

Foreword

Though it might sound more than a little trite, a lot has changed in the airline world since 1970.

To start with the obvious, two of the then-eleven US trunk carriers flew their last piston engine-powered flights then. First was United, using a Douglas DC-6B to serve points in eastern Nevada for the last time on February 28, 1970. Presaging what was to come, the Douglas would be replaced by a Convair 580, operated by Frontier Airlines on behalf of United as a "substitute" service.

Delta retired its last piston-powered aircraft, the Convair 440, on April 25, 1970. Then, the local service carriers, now beginning to think of themselves as "regional" carriers, got in on the act. Piedmont, for example, flew its last scheduled Martin 404 flight fourteen days before the United milestone, on Valentine's Day, although Southern Airways would continue using this equipment type until April 30, 1978.

The big news in the airline industry in 1970 vis-à-vis aircraft was at the other end of the size spectrum, however, in the form of Boeing's new behemoth 747, which entered service on January 22, 1970, on Pan American's New York-London route.

Before going further, it is worth adding a comment about concentrating on the aircraft used by airlines. There obviously are many other "moving parts" of these companies, ranging from passenger service to maintenance, but aircraft are the *sine qua non* of this industry; if they don't take off (and land again after a decent interval), literally nothing happens in this business.

Because of the advent of the 747, in 1970 airlines devoted much of their marketing and promotional efforts to the new type. Travelers wanted to fly on the new airliner, and others showed up at airports just to see them.

Other changes were in store as the decade progressed. Three other wide-body types appeared during the 1970s: the McDonnell Douglas DC-10, Lockheed L-1011 Tristar, and Airbus A300, the last from a newly-formed manufacturing consortium in Europe.

However, there would be bumps in the road. The most serious came in 1973/74, first with the embargo on petroleum products, the result of the so-called Yom Kippur War in October 1973. While this was relatively brief, it constrained fuel supply to such an extent that fuel for aircraft was difficult to source in some locations, and sometimes could not be obtained at all.

The long-term outcome of this was a sudden, dramatic rise in the price of petroleum products, including jet fuel. This made the economics of some of the early jets (the

Convair 880 being an example) essentially impossible. At the same time, it became clear, from a supply-and-demand perspective, that there were too many 747s in service. As we will see, while there were certain ways to ameliorate this problem, it is likely that aircraft designers and marketers had failed to anticipate that such a situation might occur, including the airlines that had participated in the frenzy of initial orders for the type.

In addition, since higher fuel prices applied to motor vehicle fuels as well, this tended to put a damper on demand for air travel, as consumers struggled to both fill their gasoline tanks and figure out where the money was going to come from to pay for the increased cost of essential transportation needs like getting to and from work.

This storm was weathered, however, and airline industry prospects improved as the decade progressed. New airports came into service in both the US (the geographically gigantic Dallas Fort Worth facility in Texas, as well as Kansas City, Missouri's Mid-Continent International (MCI)) and overseas (Narita in Tokyo and Charles de Gaulle in Paris). In addition, there were other airport projects undertaken that would bear fruit in the 1980s, such as the new terminal complex in Atlanta, Georgia.

It might seem odd, since the smaller (at the time) 737 eventually overtook it, becoming the world's most produced airliner for many years, but the tri-jet 727 was the darling of the airways in the 1970s, including the addition of customers like Air Canada and Delta (who would become the largest operator of the type) that had eschewed it following its EIS (entry into service), in 1964, until the 1970s.

While it did not get underway until the late 1970s, "deregulation," occurring first in the US (a quick definition of its essentials is that airlines began to be able to decide which markets they wanted to serve and how much to charge for their services without being beholden to government regulatory authorities), had begun to change the basic airliner playing field; "new entrants" began to appear, a process that would accelerate considerably in the 1980s.

Perhaps an effective way to bridge the comparison between the early 1970s and the present is provided by my early photographic efforts at Newark, New Jersey between late 1969 and 1972. Today, EWR is a major hub for United, and service to points around the globe is provided by both UA and many foreign/international carriers. In the early 1970s, it was unusual to see more than ten or twelve active aircraft at a time, with the possible exception of peak hours in the early morning and late afternoon/evening, and all passenger flights there were domestic. When the new A and B terminals opened in 1973, this provided the facilities for additional flights, but unlike the pair of observation decks on the then-old terminal, there were none at the new facilities, rendering them unfriendly to airliner photography.

Preface

I cannot remember a time when I was not interested in transportation, probably because such a period did not occur in the sentient portion of my life. I am pretty sure that airline and railroad timetables had a great deal to do with my learning to read. Fortunately, my family enjoyed going places, both by automobile and, a number of times when I was younger, by train.

My first airline flight that I can remember occurred when I was eight, with my grandpa, on an American Airlines Convair 240. It was the only time he ever flew, and he returned home via railroad.

Unfortunately, transportation does not get much notice in a typical elementary and secondary school education in the US, nor is college significantly better. That said, my economics course on government regulation of business at least touched on transportation, since railroads were essentially the first industry to experience what has been called the "dead hand" of economic regulation.

Finally, in graduate school at Northwestern University's Transportation Center, I found courses that were actually focused on transportation, along with other kindred spirits with whom to discuss these matters, as well as to engage in outings to see and photograph the cornucopia of Chicago's transportation entities. For my thesis topic, I would choose the airline-fleet planning process.

My photography of trains and planes began with a Kodak "Brownie" camera around the time of that first trip on the American 240, and continued through my high school years and beyond, almost exclusively in black and white until 1970. Up until this time, for a variety of reasons, I had not been paying much attention to airlines, such that when my interest was rekindled, I found out that I had largely missed out on the piston-to-jet transition period.

Along with this renewed interest in airlines, I also made the decision to work in that industry. Now photographing essentially in color (airlines were colorful, whereas Penn Central Railroad, which dominated my home territory, painted its locomotives black), I decided to see if I could make a living in the transportation field, hence the selection of Northwestern's transportation program.

Thus far, fifty-plus years later, it seems to have worked. While not all my professional activities at two airlines, two aircraft manufacturers and later, consulting, were aircraft-specific (including how to put these machines to work to produce revenue and minimize cost), these activities did make up a substantial component of my work experience. And as we will see later, a camera often accompanied me on my travels, whether for business or pleasure, which is to say that all the photos in this book are the author's.

While this book addresses the decade of the 1970s, my "serious" airline photography began in 1969, so there will be a brief digression into the previous decade, after which the main event commences.

Finally, a word about photo selection. In a work of this size, there is room for only so many photos, meaning there were many others available that I was not able to include.

I have tried to balance the typical and the unusual in telling the story of airline aircraft during the 1970s, and hope that you will find lots to enjoy within these pages and will excuse the necessary omission of those that did not make the cut.

Contents

Chapter 1

1969

N8019U, the *DC-8 Jet Mainliner W. E. Rhoades*, is departing from the terminal building at New York's JFK International Airport, then shared by United and Delta, in August 1969. Built originally as a Series 10 and delivered in November 1959, it was converted to Series 20 standards in 1966. The tail of another DC-8 of similar vintage from the United fleet can be seen behind the gate concourse at the right. Pending arrival of the first 747s in less than six months, the DC-8 and Boeing 707 were still the rulers of the airline sky at this time, although the "stretched" versions of the DC-8 (series 61/62/63) could claim pride of place in the overall size category.

Above: Although it bore the lowest registration number in Delta's Convair 880 fleet, N8801E, line number four, was delivered to the Georgia-based airline in December 1961, well after the arrival of N8802E, line number 7, in January 1960. Delta, like United, had also ordered the Douglas DC-8-10 for its longer-haul, higher-capacity jet services, but opted to acquire the four-engine CV-880 for smaller markets and where less range (not transcontinental) was required. It is seen here in August 1969 at JFK still in its basically white fuselage livery (although no longer on the belly), complete with Delta's signature "Golden Crown" emblem on both the tail and the forward fuselage.

Opposite above: As of November 27, 1969, I was in Virginia's Shenandoah Valley at Roanoke, Virginia's Woodrum Field, a major operational point for Piedmont Airlines. Originally delivered to TWA as the *Skyliner Cleveland* in August 1952, N40433 was acquired by Piedmont in December 1961. Consistent with PI's practice, it bore the *Tidewater Pacemaker* nomenclature utilizing regional place names. By late 1969, piston-powered aircraft did not have long to serve in PI's scheduled service fleet.

Opposite below: Back in the New York City area for the Christmas / New Year holidays on December 21, 1969, I was able to photograph Braniff's 727-27C (convertible-to-freighter configuration), N7276, from the east observation deck at Newark, New Jersey. Delivered in October 1966, its "End of the Plain Plane" pastel light-green livery looked like it was in need of a "refresh" after a little over three years in service. In July 1968, my first-ever jet flight was on another BN 727 (red), operating EWR-DCA-BNA (Newark Airport-Washington National Airport-Nashville Municipal Airport).

PIEDMONT
N40433

BRANIFF INTERNATIONAL
BI
N7276

Chapter 2

1970

Above: As the 1970s began, I returned to ROA on January 17, where Eastern's DC-9-14 (a "baby" Series 10 model), N8904E, was paying a brief visit. Interestingly, the original and smallest version of the DC-9 lacked the "high-lift" wing devices of the later, and larger, Series 30 models, which limited the smaller version's performance at some airports.

Opposite above: ROA as of the early 1970s was a marvelous place to see (and photograph) airliners "up close and personal," since all passenger traffic was handled at ground-level outdoor gates sans boarding bridges or, for that matter, anything to impede the view. Here, Piedmont's 737-200 *Outer Banks Pacemaker*, N747N, is being prepared for departure, in the process illustrating how the integral forward airstair is stowed in the fuselage below the forward entry door.

Opposite below: A March 1970 visit to Roanoke's Woodrum Field found PI's Martin 404, N40413, posing by the company hangar, and in the process depicting the Martin's signature ventral air stairs. However, the type's role at Piedmont has now shifted, as the airline's final regular 404 service had taken place on Valentine's Day, February 14, 1970. Now it and a modest number of its compatriots are in charter service only, bringing an end to Piedmont's use of piston-powered aircraft in its scheduled service.

PIEDMONT AIRLINES
OUTER BANKS PACEMAKER
747
SHELL

FLY
AIRLINES
PIEDMONT
N4041
PIEDMONT AIRLINES

Above: By the date of this April 1, 1970, shot at New York's LaGuardia Airport, at the Eastern Air Lines Shuttle terminal, all of the regular-service/first-section flights had been assigned to a group of EA's DC-9-30s; N8927E is getting an inspection by the first officer assigned to this trip. Lockheed L-188 "Electra" turboprops now comprised the reserve/extra-section fleet, and would continue to do so for most of the 1970s.

Opposite above: Over at LGA's main terminal, TWA's 727-31, N852TW, is boarding its outbound passengers via the rear/ventral airstair, indicating that this gate did not have an enclosed boarding bridge. The aircraft still wears its "StarStream 727" titles on the number three engine's nacelles, a practice carried over from the carrier's later, fan-powered Boeing 707s.

Opposite below: Across the Hudson River at EWR, American Airlines' Boeing 720-023B, N7545A, sits outside the AA Hanger in April 1970. The long since demolished set of maintenance facilities seen here advertises numerous now-vanished airlines. However, of those listed, only one—Eastern—did not end up being incorporated into today's American Airlines, including TWA, Allegheny and Mohawk.

TWA
TWA

AMERICAN AIRLINES
American

Above: This view of Eastern's 727-25 N8123N at Roanoke on March 17, 1970, illustrates that the 727-100's design approach to stowing the forward integral airstair was less convoluted than that of the 737-200 that we observed at the same location earlier in the year.

Opposite above: A June 4, 1970, visit to HPN, the airport for White Plains, New York (although the facility's eastern boundary abuts the Connecticut state line) provided this view of a pair of Mohawk's BAC (British Aircraft Corporation)-111 twin jet airliners. At the time MO was the exclusive provider of scheduled airline service at this location, utilizing turboprop FH-227s in addition to the 200-series jets seen here.

Opposite below: As a replacement for its remaining L-188 turboprop Electras, American Airlines chose the 400-Series of the BAC-111, beginning in late 1965. By this time, AA had taken to calling its fan-jet fleet "Astrojets" and thus referred to its BAC fleet as "400 Astrojets," possibly in an attempt to differentiate its product from Mohawk's use of the "earlier" -200 series on routes to and from upstate New York, where both airlines competed directly. In any case, the Series-400s did not last long at American, with their disposal from that fleet beginning in the early 1970s. N5043 is at LGA on June 14, 1970; by January 1972 it will be gone from the AA fleet.

N1118J
MOHAWK

N5043
AMERICAN AIRLINES
400 ASTROJET
TEXACO
SERVING AMERICAN AIRLINES
ESSO

Above: In June 1970, I began a career in the commercial aviation business when I joined TWA (Trans World Airlines) as a part-time/seasonal customer service agent at the airline's iconic "Saarinen Terminal" at JFK Airport. As such, the Boeing 747 and I entered into regular service in the airline industry during the same year, albeit with the aircraft a few months ahead of me. After undergoing a training course (it was not every day that you could find someone willing to pay you to learn how to use the OAG (Official Airline Guide)) and acclimating to the job, which took place at the ticket counter and the boarding gates, I eventually was able to venture onto the ramp for some photography during my first summer there. Here is a view of N93101 having its lavatory service performed by the "honey wagon." Notice how shiny the bare metal still is!

Opposite above: In the summer of 1970, Convair 880s, operated by both Delta and TWA, could still be seen at JFK. Here, N810TW has been pushed back from the gate and appears to be awaiting the loading of a last-minute piece of baggage before departing for Dayton, Ohio. For that matter, prior to Northeast Airlines' acquisition of 727-200s, the CV880s they used in the New York-Florida market were regular visitors to JFK also.

Opposite below: Delivered in May 1959, N739TW was one of the "original" non-fan engine 707-131s intended for domestic long-haul service. As of September 4, 1970, it was considered "geriatric" at eleven years of age, and by 1972, all of these aircraft were removed from the fleet. That is the distinctive shape of the Saarinen Terminal in the background.

TWA
N810TW
TWA

TWA

Above: Due to their early jet-engine technology, airplanes like N739TW were given the nickname "Water Wagons," since they utilized a water/alcohol mixture at takeoff in an attempt to get better takeoff performance by lowering combustion temperatures; newer, fan-powered engines obviated the need for this cumbersome apparatus.

Opposite above: In the early fall of 1970, I left my summer job at TWA to enroll in graduate school and study transportation in the Chicago area. It was not long before I paid a visit to O'Hare airport on the city's northwest side. A pair of observation decks at ORD provided good views of much of the airside, including local service carrier North Central's extensive operations, which featured a mix of turboprop Convair 580s and pure-jet Douglas DC-9-30s.

Opposite below: On the other side of the terminal, United's DC-8-20 N8025U is taxiing to its gate at ORD on September 12, 1970. Like TWA's N739TW, this early-1960 delivery will not be in United's fleet much longer. In the background are a DC-9-30, 727-200 and a "stretched" DC-8-61 belonging to Eastern Airlines.

NORTH CENTRAL
NORTH CENTRAL

UNITED
N8025U
UNITED

Above: Although United had elected to cast its early large-jet lot with the Douglas DC-8, the carrier's management soon decided that they also needed a somewhat smaller four-engine jet for shorter and smaller markets. Boeing was happy to oblige by producing a shortened version of the 707 for this purpose but chose to name this product the 720 in order to spare United the embarrassment of purchasing the same type they had earlier eschewed in favor of the DC-8. American, which had gone for the 707 in the first place, apparently had no qualms about adding the 720 to its fleet, but unlike United, opted to install fanjet engines on its versions, which N7227U clearly lacks.

Opposite above: In 1969, United opted for a modest fleet of the (slightly) stretched DC-8-62, with N8974 seen arriving at its departure gate on October 1, 1970. At this point United's primary use of this specific, very long-range type involved, primarily, the airline's service to Hawaii, in particular the nonstop between Chicago and Honolulu.

Opposite below: United was the only US airline to acquire the French-built twin-jet Caravelle new from the manufacturer, assembling a fleet of twenty of the type, which it used on shorter-distance routes, especially in the eastern portion of its route structure. By October 1, 1970, when this shot was taken, the Caravelle fleet was in an all-first class configuration that was well-suited for what had been the carrier's "Executive Service" operation between Chicago and Newark (the type was not operated routinely to and from La Guardia in New York City). Among other features, it provided "men only" service; this meant steak dinners and onboard cigar-smoking. However, at this point, it has been reduced to operating a mid-morning nonstop to South Bend, Indiana, still with only F-class seats, of course.

UNITED
UNITED
EASTERN

UNITED
N1009U
UNITED

Above: A more common sight at a Chicago airport by the early 1970s, of course, was a United 727-100. This one, N7058U, on October 17, 1970, is seen at Midway Airport, on Chicago's Southwest Side. Interestingly, the building to the right was once United's corporate headquarters, and in the 1980s would serve the same function for the deregulation "upstart" carrier Midway Airlines.

Opposite above: An outcome of the US military presence in Southeast Asia during the late 1960s and early 1970s was the growth of a group of non-scheduled airlines known as "supplemental" carriers in the parlance of the then economically regulated US airline business. These companies participated extensively in airlifting troops and cargo involved in what would become the Vietnam War, and these contracts enabled them to finance large, long-range aircraft. As the war eventually wound down, some of them found their way into non-scheduled "charter" services, serving the civilian market at lower prices. This World Airways 707-320C is at ORD on December 2, 1970.

Opposite below: In addition to its modest DC-8-62 fleet, United also invested in the longer DC-8-61 model, which lacked the extreme range of the -62, or -63 models. But at this point (December 5, 1970) UA did not get farther from the continental US than the Hawaiian Islands, so it choose to capitalize on the lower operating cost of the -61 without expending capital on range that it did not need in the late 1960s. Here, N8091U is seen arriving at ORD runway 27R.

WORLD AIRWAYS
707C

UNITED
N8091U
UNITED

Above: Christmas break 1970 featured a trip to a warmer climate, specifically southeast Florida, which offered the chance to see the many interesting and, in some cases, exotic aviation activities featured at Miami International Airport. Here, on December 27, 1970, Braniff's DC-8-62, N1804, is parked at its MIA gate, with the in-terminal International Hotel as a backdrop. At this time, BN was operating virtually all of its long-haul South American route system with a fleet of seven examples of the Douglas long-haul type.

Opposite above: OB-R-765 has been pushed back in preparation for departure of its APSA (Aerolineas Peruanas SA) flight to Peru at MIA on December 27, 1970. Interestingly, this example of the relatively rare type (of the thirty-seven built, twenty-five went to American Airlines, initially) had its first airline service at APSA.

Opposite below: Although its "corporate" head office then was in New York City's Rockefeller Center, its operating headquarters was on the northeast corner of MIA. Here, we see a pair of stretched DC-8s, a DC-9-30, and a "Whisper Whale" in the background, on December 27, 1970. We will take a better look at the latter coming up in a few months!

APSA
AEROLINEAS PERUANAS
64

EASTERN
EASTERN

By late 1970, the bulk of Northeast Airlines' long-haul service was being provided by Boeing 727-200s; the airline was the first carrier to operate the "stretched" model of the popular type in December 1967. Here, N1646 exhibits the distinctive "Yellowbird" livery, which NE had adopted in 1966. In the days before "smokeless burner cans" on the type's JT8D engines, it is easy to see how the description of the color scheme often morphed into "Dirtybird" territory.

Chapter 3

1971

While Pan American's initial jet order skewed towards the Douglas DC-8 (twenty-five) as opposed to the Boeing 707 (twenty), the latter type eventually won out. By 1970 PAA was no longer operating DC-8s… Or was it? And why would Pan Am have acquired a single example of the DC-8-62, as seen at MIA on January 1, 1971?

What we are looking at here is a vestige of history, in the form of an interchange service between Pan Am and Braniff dating back to before Braniff's acquisition of Panagra Airlines in 1967. N1803 is in fact a Braniff aircraft, operated by Braniff crews. But Pan Am, in those days, still had clout, and was considered second-most popular American brand behind Coca-Cola.

Above: All three major forms of airliner engines in a single shot: the piston-powered Aviateca DC-6B; Eastern's turboprop L-188 Electra; APSA's jet/turbine (in this case, aft-fan powered) CV-990A at MIA on January 3, 1971.

Opposite above: Braniff's N7289, in the pastel yellow "jellybean" or "Easter Egg" livery, arriving at ORD on January 24, 1971. Amazingly, given the relatively brutal winter weather during that month in Chicagoland, no snow is visible.

Opposite below: "Combi" long-haul operations, with both passenger accommodations and cargo space on the main deck, did not arrive with the use of this operating practice during the early years of the 747. Here is a 1971 example utilizing KLM's DC-8-50 PH-DCU on January 24, 1971, at ORD. On 707s and DC-8s, the main-deck cargo was carried in the forward portion of the fuselage (due to the location of the cargo door), while passengers rode behind the freight. This necessitated the use of narrower cargo pallets, since the flight-deck crew had to be able to get from the cockpit to the passenger section if needed.

BI
BRANIFF INTERNATIONAL

KLM
ROYAL DUTCH AIRLINES
PH-DCU

Above: A February 24, 1971, return visit to Virginia's Shenandoah Valley finds a pair of Piedmont 737s exchanging passengers at Roanoke.

Opposite above: Two days later, on February 26, finds N737N, PI's *Chesapeake Pacemaker*, departing under more pleasant weather conditions.

Opposite below: During my visit to Miami International between Christmas and New Year's, I had shot a photo with an Eastern 747 in the distance. Now, on March 24, 1971, at New York's JFK, here is a closer look at another one, this time in a somewhat different livery. When the 747 was launched, Eastern Airlines, like most of the other US "trunk" carriers signed up for four. However, once the DC-10 and L-1011 widebody tri-jets came on the market, EA concluded that these were of a more appropriate size for their route system and ordered the Lockheed product. (TWA ended up taking the four 747 delivery positions vacated by Eastern.) However, due to the bankruptcy of the L-1011's engine supplier, Rolls-Royce, the entry into service of the type was delayed by a year, from 1971 to 1972. Since Eastern had planned to have widebody capacity for the winter season in 1971, it leased three 747s from Pan Am to cover this capacity shortfall. One of the aircraft received the full EA "Hockey Stick" livery. As we can see from this photo of N731PA during its tour of duty with Eastern, it remained largely in its Pan Am paint scheme, only with Eastern titles.

PIEDMONT
N737N
PIEDMONT AIRLINES

EASTERN
EASTERN

Above: As of March 1971, the largest aircraft in Eastern's own fleet were its DC-8s, including a modest number of Series 61s and 63s, along with its original DC-8-20s from the dawn of the jet age. N8603 was part of the latter category and is shown being pushed back from its departure gate. In the background, at United's JFK terminal, are other DC-8s of similar vintage, as well as a then new 747.

Opposite above: Trans Caribbean Airways had long been a competitor of both Eastern and Pan American in the northeast-Puerto Rico market and, like Eastern, relied on early-model DC-8s for much of their capacity, including its DC-8-50, N8785R. What is different in this photo is that the TCA aircraft is at the American Airlines terminal at JFK on March 24, 1971. Note the AA 747 to its rear. As of March 2, 1971, TCA was acquired by American, and the DC-8s were quickly disposed of by AA, which provided useful opportunities for some of American's numerous (sixteen) 747s, particularly on its JFK-San Juan route.

Opposite below: Arriving at JFK on March 24, 1971, is this Air Canada Viscount 700, CF-TIF. AC shared the then new terminal served by BOAC (and later, British Airways). At this point, all of the Canadian carrier's New York City service was at JFK, rather than the closer-to-midtown La Guardia Airport. Most of AC's services were to Montreal and Toronto, but as seen here, there was a daily flight providing service to the Canadian Maritime provinces, via Halifax, Nova Scotia, that continued to use the Vickers turboprop in lieu of the DC-9-30s then utilized for Air Canada's New York-Ontario/Quebec services.

TRANS CARIB
N8785R

AIR CANADA
CF-TIF
650

Above: A return visit to JFK on March 29, 1971, provided this view of N735PA, which was painted in Eastern's full colors (likely for publicity purposes) during its winter-season lease from Pan Am.

Opposite above: On my return trip to Chicago from New York in spring 1971, I took a slight detour to the Port Clinton airport in northwestern Ohio (now the Erie-Ottawa International Airport) to see this anachronism on March 31. N7684 had been built as a Ford model 4-AT-B in 1928, and beyond all reason, was still in scheduled service five decades later.

Opposite below: As we see here, both passengers and freight are being loaded aboard the Ford Tri-motor, in what was not only an intra-state operation (thus avoiding federal economic regulation), but also an intra-county entity, since its principal destination, out of Port Clinton, was the town of Put-in-Bay on South Bass Island in the US portion of Lake Erie, meaning both points were located in Ohio's Ottawa County.

LINES

Above: On a road trip in early April 1971, I noticed what appeared to be a purple airplane as I passed by Indianapolis's Weir Cook Airport. On my return trip on April 22, I had the time to stop and take a better look (along with a photo for posterity). In 1968, Allegheny Airlines acquired and merged with fellow local service carrier Lake Central. In geographic terms, this was an "end-to-end" merger, since their service territories were essentially contiguous. Lake Central had acquired a fleet of French-built Nord 262 turboprops, including N26203.

Opposite above: Subsequent to the merger, Allegheny decided to emphasize the French *provenance* of the aircraft by giving each one a French-sounding female name (this one is *Nicole d'ALLEGHENY*) and ditched Lake Central's bland white/red/blue colors for this regal purple livery, with a broad gold stripe and fleur-de-lis for good measure. It is not apparent that this produced significant new traffic in former LCA service points like Findlay, Ohio and Martinsburg, West Virginia. In fact, as we can see here, the three French ladies at IND (Lake Central's former headquarters) are parked out of service. In contrast to current airport security practices, I searched in vain for someone to give me permission to photograph these airplanes before concluding that it would be easier to simply walk through the wide-open gate, which no sign or placard prohibited.

Opposite below: Back at ORD on May 1, 1971, this photo was hard to resist, since N607US had provided me with my very first 747 ride in December 1970, from ORD to JFK, the tail end of a TYO-SEA-ORD-JFK itinerary. One of Northwest Orient's original 10 747-100s, it is still in the original "three-window" (on each side) configuration on the upper deck. This location was, of course, fenced, but it was easy to shoot over the fence for views such as this.

N607US
NORTHWEST ORIENT

Above: By July 8, 1971, I was back at work at the TWA JFK Flight Center for the summer. What to do on your days off, which were typically mid-week? A visit to EWR was in order, where I found Eastern's Electra N5504 being guided into its gate, with another of the type on the ramp to the rear.

Opposite above: Part of the reason for the Newark visit was that my then future father-in-law, E. B. "Ernie" Hummel, was in command of the Braniff 720, N7080, shown here departing for Dallas, and we were able to briefly meet during the aircraft's EWR layover. Apparently, Braniff pilots thought that these non-fan engine aircraft were somewhat underpowered, derisively describing them as "powered by Evinrude" (a manufacturer of outboard motors for small boats).

Opposite below: During my second "JFK summer," I worked occasionally at TWA's ticket counter in the IAB (International Arrivals Building). Much of my work entailed re-directing people who had come to meet passengers they had expected to arrive at the IAB to the TWA terminal, since the airline's international flights arrived there, as of 1970. One advantage was the opportunity to take my meal break on what was left of the IAB's once-extensive rooftop observation deck. The aircraft being pushed back is one of Pan Am's original 707-120s, now upgraded with fan engines. Originally, N710PA was the *Clipper America*; it is now the *Clipper Caroline*, since N747PA (yes, the type and registration are the same) now carries the *America* nomenclature.

BI
BRANIFF INTERNATIONAL
N7080

NE
PAN AMERICAN

Above: Allegheny Airlines was on the (upward) move as of this view of its DC-9-30, N963VJ (VJ standing for "Vista Jet"), at LGA on August 25, 1971. As we have seen previously, AL had acquired fellow local service carrier Lake Central in 1968, expanding its route network into the Midwest. Another chessboard move will add to its presence in the Northeast in 1972. AL was in the process of turning Pittsburgh into a hub, and displacing TWA's historic position in the Steel City. Incidentally, this aircraft was one of seventy-five that the carrier would eventually add to its fleet.

Opposite above: Over at JFK's IAB on September 4, 1971, is evidence of both the past—in terms of Pan Am 747s inbound from overseas, since what will become Pan Am's "Worldport" will not open until 1972, relieving the airline of the need to transfer aircraft back to the Pan Am terminal for departure—and the future—in the form of the 707 with the "Caledonian/BUA" titles, reflecting the recent merger of the Scottish/English (British United) air carriers.

Opposite below: By September 1971, I had accumulated enough hours at TWA to be eligible for a limited amount of "free and reduced rate "air transportation for personal use. Since I had a great desire to upgrade my camera from the Argus C-3 "Brick" I had been using to a Nikon SLR (single-lens reflex), this turned into a trip to Tokyo on Pan Am (via Fairbanks, Alaska on 707s). Since the photo equipment that I purchased in Japan cost about 40 percent of what it retailed for in the US, I essentially got camera gear and a trip to Japan for the same amount of money. I put the new camera and lenses to good, albeit modest, use at Tokyo's Haneda airport on my way home on September 15, 1971, capturing KLM's short-lived use of Aeroflot IL-62s on its trans-Siberian route between Europe and Japan, as well as an All Nippon Airways 727-200 and a Pan Am 747 in the background.

PAN AM
CALEDONIAN // BUA

全日空
ALL NIPPON AIRWAYS
JA8328
ALL NIPPON AIRWAYS CO.LTD
KLM
JAL
JAL

Above: A visit to San Francisco in September 1971 following my trip to Japan brought a number of new subjects in front of my Nikon's viewfinder, and now, with a medium telephoto lens, more distant subjects could be addressed. I had never seen either PSA (Pacific Southwest Airlines) or Air West (assembled from previous local service carriers Bonanza, Pacific and West Coast) prior to my SFO visit on September 21. The patches of color on the Air West aircraft brought to mind Braniff's use of multicolor airplanes, albeit on a more modest scale.

Below: At the other end of the airliner size spectrum, I was able to capture these two American Airlines 747s eyeing each other between trips, also on September 21, 1971.

The Air West graphics definitely had a bold look, along with mix-and-match colors. Both looked good on the turboprop F-27 equipment as well as the DC-9 jets in the airline's employ.

Above: Early the next month, on October 1, 1970, I traveled from Chicago to Louisville, Kentucky (as a pass rider, the long way around, via Kansas City, Missouri), where I found this pair of Convair 880s representing TWA and Delta, respectively, the latter showing the long-lived Delta livery that began with the deliveries of DC-8-50s to the Atlanta-based carrier in the mid-1960s.

Opposite above: I have been asked many times if anything unusual is happening here as N809TW comes to a stop after landing on ORD runway 27R on November 4, 1971. The answer is nothing. This is a CV-880 using reverse thrust; this produced a copious display of what appears to be partially combusted jet fuel.

Opposite below: Shortly after the 880's smoky arrival, Continental's 747-124, N26864, arrived on the same runway with considerably less visual evidence of fuel, burned or otherwise. CO used the tag "The Proud Bird with the Golden Tail" to describe their equipment. There certainly is a lot of gold paint on that tail, to say the least!

TWA
TWA

CONTINENTAL

Above: Christmas break 1971 found me back at MIA on December 27, where I captured this view of multiple Eastern Airlines aircraft, including DC-9s, 727s, an Electra, and one of the 747s leased from Pan Am, in full EA colors.

Opposite above: Also present at MIA on December 27, 1971, was this Braniff dark green 707-327C, which I believe was operating a charter in conjunction with the Orange Bowl football game coming up in the Dade County (Florida) metropolis.

Opposite below: The northwest corner of the Miami Airport, along NW 36th Street, was a location that often featured parked aircraft not currently in use. This, combined with the humid climate in southern coastal Florida, resulted in the nickname "Corrosion Corner," particularly applicable to older aircraft with little prospect of near-term (if any) future use. A pair of former Eastern Constellations, along with a Convair 440 from the same company, is working hard on their suntans on December 28, 1971.

BRANIFF INTERNATIONAL
TEXACO

N6205C

Chapter 4

1972

Above: On the second day of 1972, one of National Airlines' pair of DC-8-61s—N45191—is about to depart Newark on its way to Miami, Florida. Notice the name "Christine" on the right forward fuselage; this was part of the airline's "Fly Me" advertising campaign of this era, which featured pictures of individual female National Airlines flight attendants and the tagline "Fly Me; I'm [flight attendant's name]." This was supposedly an attempt to personalize the service being offered.

Opposite above: This 707-138B model, now N108BN, was one of a group of unique 707-120 model aircraft for the Australian Airline Qantas. These aircraft were about 10ft. shorter than other 707-120s, and for that matter, were slightly shorter than Boeing's 720 aircraft. Braniff acquired four of these in the late 1960s. This one can be seen at EWR on January 2, 1972. Later it would be acquired by the American actor John Travolta, who used it as his personal aircraft, bearing the registration N707JT.

Opposite below: Also at EWR on January 2, 1972, is TWA's 707-331B N18711. This aircraft is operating in a high-capacity all-coach seating configuration in TWA's charter fleet for an "inclusive tour" product for a local travel company, serving the EWR-Las Vegas market on Sundays and Thursdays, thus creating alternating three- and four-day packages in this market.

BI
BRANIFF INTERNATIONAL

TWA
MOHAWK
AMERICAN AIRLI
TWA

Above: Still at Newark on January 2, 1972, lots of history visible here: what became the airport's "North" Terminal, with its predecessor visible to the right; an FH-227 and BAC-111 in the "old" Mohawk colors; and the World Trade Center's Twin Towers in lower Manhattan under construction in the distance.

Opposite above: Here is a closer look at the "old" Newark Terminal, to the east of the one that replaced it. Looks like a good crowd is enjoying the view from the observation deck, including an Eastern Electra, Mohawk BAC-111, and Allegheny Commuter Beech 99.

Opposite below: As the sun sets on January 2, 1972, Delta's DC-8-51, N814E, makes a dramatic entry, with the Port Newark shipping facilities as a backdrop.

EASTERN
N336PL
ALLEGHENY
M O

DELTA

Above: Another visit to EWR on January 23, 1972, yielded this shot of a red Braniff 727-91, which the colorful carrier added to its roster in late 1969, following the aircraft's initial service with Frontier Airlines between October 1966 and December 1969.

Opposite above: Also on January 23, we can see the WTC's Twin Towers are further along in their construction, along with the Mohawk's new "Buckskin" paint scheme on N1136J, with N1123J behind providing a comparison with the previous livery.

Opposite below: One week later, on January 30, 1972, a wide variety of aircraft are in view at La Guardia, including FH227s both from Mohawk, in the background, and a Northeast "Yellowbird" version closer to the camera.

MOHAWK

NE
N378NE
SHELL

Above: A long-held goal of visiting London's Heathrow Airport was fulfilled on the President's Day Holiday on February 21, 1972. By this time I had joined TWA full time in its 3rd Avenue headquarters in Manhattan and thus was able to use my free travel privileges on a space-available / standby basis. An office friend and I flew east on Sunday evening to LHR, and returned to JFK approximately twenty-four hours later. While I would have preferred better weather and lighting conditions, it was still thrilling to see this lineup of Hawker-Siddeley Tridents in the "Union Jack tail" livery at their gates in Terminal One.

Opposite above: Interestingly, Ireland's Aer Lingus occupied the closest, most convenient gate to the terminal on this side of the building for its service to Dublin; however no covered boarding bridge seems to be available for this location.

Opposite below: Over at Terminal Two, also known then as the "Europa" building, this trio of DC-9-30s was providing services between London and other European points as far apart as the Iberian Peninsula and the Bosporus.

AER LINGUS IRISH INTERNATIONAL
BOEING 737
EI-ASF
G-AWZH
BEA
Trident Three

IBERIA LINEAS AEREAS DE ESPAÑA
DC-9
EC-BIN
IB
TURK HAVA YOLLARI - TURKISH AIRLINES
TC-JAF
AUSTRIAN
BEA

Above: A visit to San Francisco the next weekend, on February 26, 1972, provided some now familiar equipment, in the form of a pair of PSA 727-200s, and well as something new: a Hughes Air West DC-9-14 in its bright yellow "banana" Hughes Air West livery. The re-titling reflected the airline's new owner, aviation industry titan Howard Hughes. N9104 had started its career with West Coast Airlines in 1967.

Opposite above: All dressed up, but nowhere to go. By March 1992, when I visited the TWA maintenance facility in Kansas City, the airline had retired its fleet of 707-131 "Water Wagons" and made attempts to market these aircraft to other carriers. This pair got as far as being painted for Air Manila International, including the application of Philippine civil registrations (e.g., PIC-7072). The former TWA registration, N741TW, is still partially visible above the new/prospective version. In the end, the deal did not go through, and the paint job was for naught.

Opposite below: TWA was also attempting to sell its pair of Lockheed "Jetstar" business aircraft acquired for pilot training, the theory being that a smaller aircraft would have lower costs than regular, full-size aircraft. One of the Jetstars was configured to represent a Boeing 707, and the other, a Boeing 727. Even in the early 1970s, simulator technology was advancing rapidly and would eventually result in type ratings for pilots upgrading to a new/different type of aircraft that could be issued without any cockpit time in an actual aircraft.

AMI
Air Manila International
PIC-7072

TWA
TWA
N7963S
TWA

Above: By March 9, 1972, I had the opportunity to revisit Heathrow on what proved to be a nice spring day. This time an Aer Lingus BAC-111 is occupying that close ramp space at Terminal One, and the lineup of BEA "Union Jack Tridents" behind it is interrupted by a Vickers Vanguard turboprop that is still in the previous "Red Square" tail livery.

Opposite above: Swissair was the second largest original customer for the Convair 990, with a fleet of eight examples, following the twenty-five that went to American Airlines initially. HB-ICF is seen here arriving at Heathrow's Terminal 2 on March 19, 1972. The upcoming 1973/74 oil crisis that caused aviation fuel prices to soar would see the 990s exiting the Swissair fleet by the mid-1970s. However, one example (-ICC) is preserved in the Swiss Museum of Transport in Lucerne/Luzern.

Opposite below: British European Airways (BEA) Trident 1C is front and center at Terminal One at LHR on March 9. Also visible in the far background is a Trident 2 of Cyprus Airways.

SWISSAIR
CORONADO
HB-ICF

BEA
G-ARPZ
Trident
G-AWZB
Trident Three

Above: Here is a look at the ramp at Zurich, Switzerland's Kloten Airport on the pleasant Sunday afternoon of April 9, 1972. Swissair's DC-9-32, HB-IFL, is most prominent, with the airline's DC-8-62, HB-IDL, behind it. Other aircraft present include an Aeroflot IL-62, an SAS DC-9, and a Spantax Convair 990. The most interesting aircraft pictured, however, is TWA's 707-331B, N28714, which will soon depart ZRH for JFK via GVA (Geneva) as TWA flight 833. Originally registered N776TW, its cockpit was destroyed on the ground by a bomb in Damascus, Syria in August 1969. The aircraft was subsequently rebuilt, with a new nose supplied by Boeing, and re-entered service in December 1969 with the same registration seen here.

Opposite above: Swissair's initial pair of 747-200s are visible here at Zurich on April 9, 1972: HB-IGA and -IGB. Both will be operating to New York City's JFK airport: one nonstop, the other via Geneva. In the absence of enclosed boarding bridges, at least modest overhead protection is provided to passengers as they make the significant ascent to the 747's main deck.

Opposite below: This IL-62, SU-ARO, at Frankfurt, West Germany on April 29, 1972, is now wearing EgyptAir titles. Between 1958 and 1971, however, there had been a political alliance between Egypt and Syria, which titled itself the United Arab Republic. Historically, EgyptAir had been known as Misrair prior to the formation of the UAR; during the period when the two companies were allied their airline was United Arab Airlines. At the time of the breakup in 1971, the name EgyptAir was adopted for the Egyptian component. EgyptAir had the distinction of operating both Boeing 707s and USSR Ilyushin products simultaneously.

SWISSAIR

EGYPTAIR
SU-ARO

Above: Northeast's DC-9-30, N972NE, is seen at its home base, Boston's Logan International Airport, on April 30, 1972, proudly displaying its "Yellowbird" livery. As we will see shortly, in five months both the airline and its livery will become past tense.

Below: Also arriving at BOS on April 30 is the first example of BOAC's (British Overseas Airways Corporation) 747 fleet, G-AWNA. Although it was delivered to the British carrier in April 1970, due to a dispute between the airline and its pilots over compensation, the inaugural BOAC 747 scheduled flight did not occur April 14, 1971, with G-AWNF doing the honors between LHR and JFK.

Above: Here is an interesting lineup of "foreign visitors" on JFK's north side on May 28, 1972: an Avensa DC-9-14, from Venezuela; a LAN Chile 707; and a Loftleidir Icelandic DC-8.

Below: In anticipation of obtaining long-haul international routes in the late 1960s, Eastern Airlines ordered a small number of DC-8-63 "PF" aircraft, the letter suffix indicating that these aircraft were structurally capable of being converted to long-haul freighters if desired, although they were built without large main-deck cargo doors. In any case, sans international routes, and particularly after the advent of the L-1011 in Eastern's fleet, there was little need for these "stretched" DC-8s. N8756 is seen here at JFK on May 28, 1972.

Above: Also at the Eastern Airlines JFK terminal on May 28 is evidence of the recent (April 12, 1972) merger of Allegheny and Mohawk, with AL being the surviving carrier. Former MO BAC-111 N1118J has already been repainted into Allegheny's livery and titles; the Mohawk FH-227 is still awaiting its trip to the paint shop.

Opposite above: Immediately to the east of the EA terminal was the architecturally undistinguished structure serving as the JFK terminal for Braniff, Northeast and Northwest Orient. The latter's 707-351C, N373US, is in the process of arriving.

Opposite below: Although it did not order the type directly from Boeing, Pan Am did acquire a modest group of 720Bs (the letter indicating that these aircraft were fan-powered) from both American Airlines and Lufthansa. These lower-capacity/-range versions of the 707 were used primarily in the airline's Caribbean and Latin American services. N782PA, the *Jet Clipper De Soto*, is a 720-023B acquired from American. It can be seen at what was then called Coolidge International Airport on the West Indian island of Antigua on June 19, 1972, and will depart shortly for San Juan, Puerto Rico.

NORTHWEST ORIENT
NORTHWEST
3
4

PAN AMERICAN
N782PA
PAN AM

Above: On July 28, 1972, this pair of American Airlines DC-10-10s, with N114AA in the foreground, is at La Guardia Airport in New York City. The type is coming up on its one-year anniversary of service, with American and United beginning scheduled DC-10 operations on August 5, 1971.

Opposite: Photographically, sometimes things line up just right. However, in my experience, the opportunity is often fleeting. Here is an example at LGA on July 28, 1972, with five TWA 727-31s—bracketed by N853TW and N858TW—line up for a family portrait.

TWA
N856TW
TWA
TWA
TWA
TWA
Finest food in flight
TWA
N853TW

Above: At the next concourse to the east, also on July 28, it was possible to see this collection of airplanes at gates that primarily served Eastern, with representatives from Allegheny and Piedmont also sharing the space.

Opposite above: D-ABOB is arriving at JFK's IAB on September 10, 1972. From the appearance of the nacelles on this Lufthansa 707-430, it might be tempting to place the aircraft's propulsion system in the "non-fan" category, but this would be inaccurate. In reality the -400-series 707s were powered by Rolls-Royce Conway engines, an early example of a fan-jet engine, although one with a relatively low bypass ratio.

Opposite below: The year 1972 was one for mergers in the US airline industry, as we saw earlier with Allegheny and Mohawk. On August 1, Northeast was merged into Delta, and by the time of this photo at LGA on December 10, the previous yellow livery on N378NE had morphed into the Delta "Widget" paint scheme. Prior to this merger, Delta had shunned turboprop equipment, at least for passenger service (although it had purchased Lockheed L-100 freighter aircraft using this propulsion method). This left TWA as the only domestic "trunk" line still in existence to have never utilized passenger turboprop aircraft in its own operations.

Lufthansa

DELTA
DELTA
DELTA
N378NE
005

Chapter 5

1973

Above: By the time of this scene at JFK on February 19, 1973, the leased Pan Am 747s are no longer needed by Eastern, since Lockheed started delivering L-1011s in mid-1972. Thus, N304EA and its sisters are now the "queens" of Eastern's fleet, eliminating the need for 747s even for peak-season capacity needs. In the background is JFK's IAB and control tower.

Opposite above: Delta, now ensconced in the terminal formerly used by Northeast, immediately to the east of the Eastern terminal, also had to deal with the one-year delay in Lockheed's TriStar program. But they chose a different route. DL ordered five examples of the L-1011's direct competitor, the DC-10, which was, after all, roughly the equivalent in terms of seat capacity. By the time that these aircraft were ready for delivery, in late 1972, it was apparent that the near-term problems with the L-1011 had been solved, so Delta arranged to sell their DC-10s to United, a major operator of the type. To satisfy its short-run capacity needs, and fit in with United's capacity planning, Delta arranged to lease these DC-10s back from United and operate them into 1975. Thus, Delta reached the (dubious) distinction of operating all three of the early US-built widebodies (747, DC-10, L-10011) simultaneously, as illustrated here by N602DA, also at JFK on February 19, 1973.

Opposite below: Prior to its acquisition of 747s, the entire fleet of Australia's overseas airline, Qantas, consisted of 707-338B/Cs and a pair of then relatively ancient Douglas DC-4s, needed to maintain service to Norfolk Island. A pair of narrow-body Boeing products are seen at their gates at Sydney (Kingsford Smith) Airport on April 12, 1973.

DELTA
DELTA
DELTA

QANTAS
V-JET
AUSTRALIA
QANTAS
VH-EAI
707

Above: Returning from "down under" on April 13, 1973, I had a stopover in the Hawaiian Islands and encountered this 720-047B, N3162, from the Western Airlines fleet.

Left: In 1972, Pan Am had opened its expanded "Worldport" terminal facilities at JFK, and one of its best features was the rooftop parking area, which quickly became the airport's de facto observation deck. As you can see here, it was possible to literally look into the eyes of a 747 parked at the gate, in this case N657PA on June 9, 1973.

Above: Northwest Airlines had long been famed for its frugality, including practices like not having doors on the stalls in the men's room, to discourage employees from taking reading matter into them, and thus impairing worker efficiency. As of June 1973, the airline still had a few of its 720B aircraft in service, although they clearly were on their way out of the NW fleet. It is likely that N737US had recently undergone a heavy maintenance check that would have resulted in a repaint, had it remained, so it returned to service wearing this "bare-metal" scheme. The airline still proudly included "Orient" in its titles at that point, meaning enough red paint needed to be allocated to include both words. By early 1974, the aircraft had been bought by Denmark's Maersk Air. No word on whether the deal included a paint job!

Below: On September 30, 1973, this westward view was recorded from the Pan Am roof. Both domestic (727) and international (DC-8-62) equipment was on display by Braniff, and it is apparent that Delta continues to operate the FH-227s inherited from Northeast in short-haul/regional service in the Northeast / New England areas.

Above: Approximately a week later, on October 7, I captured this view of a Braniff 727-100, now in one of the four newer two-tone "Flying Colors" schemes, along with an Airlift International DC-8-63 freighter and an Eastern TriStar landing on JFK runway 13R.

Opposite above: As 1973 ended, an industry event of major consequence occurred in Texas, when the new, immense (greater than the land area of Manhattan Island) DFW Airport, located between rival cities Dallas and Fort Worth, opened on January 13, 1974. Fortunately, I was able to pay a visit to the facility it was supposed to be replacing, Love Field, in Dallas, on December 27, 1973. This included my first sighting of Southwest Airlines, then operating a relatively small fleet of 737-200s on an intra-state route system within Texas, including N22SW.

Opposite below: Braniff was a major player at DAL, its headquarters and operating base, and there were many colorful examples extant for me to photograph using the Kodachrome film in my camera. That is BN's major maintenance facility in the background behind N425BN.

SOUTHWEST
N22SW
America

BI
BRANIFF INTERNATIONAL
N425BN

Above: Love Field was one of two airports (Honolulu being the other) where you could routinely see Braniff's then sole example of the 747, N601BN. While the company formally referred to it as 747 *Place*, it was more widely known as the "Great Pumpkin" for its orange color.

Opposite above: N94207, in Texas International Airlines' "old" paint scheme (which was "new" when the carrier changed its name from Trans Texas to TI), likely had been at DAL many, many times before it went into service with its current operator. One of seventy-five Convair 240s ordered post-World War II by American, it was converted from its original piston power to turboprop power using Rolls Royce Dart engines, becoming a Convair 600 in the process.

Opposite below: TI's newer "Lone Star" paint scheme—seen here installed on its DC-9-30, N1310T, as well as a pair of CV-600s in the background—was a far better fit with the 1970s, in my estimation.

BI
BRANIFF
TEXAS INTERNATIONAL

BI
BRANIFF
Texas International
N1310T

Chapter 6

1974

Above: Two months later, on February 17, 1974, and "across the pond" to the UK, I found myself at London's Gatwick Airport, south of Central London, to observe this Britannia Airways 737-200, as well as a Laker BAC-111, and a Dan-Air Comet behind. While Britannia may have ruled the waves, I am not sure of a trident's implications in the skies.

Opposite above: Itavia's F28-1000 is being readied for a return to its Italian home base at Geneva's Cointrin Airport on March 3, 1974. The aircraft was delivered to Itavia in 1970 and would remain in the fleet until 1984.

Opposite below: A trip to Montréal-Dorval International Airport on April 19, 1974, showed that Air Canada was still using a portion of its Viscount 700 fleet in the mid-1970s. While CF-THS would be leaving the Air Canada fleet later in the month, the good news is that this aircraft could still be seen at the Royal Aviation Museum of Western Canada, in Winnipeg, Manitoba. On the other side of the remote "Aeroquay" concourse (accessed by tunnels under the ramp from the main terminal) is a CP Air DC-8.

ITAVIA
I-TIDI
F-28

AIR CANADA
VISCOUNT

Above: To the west of the terminal at YUL, I found a pair of CPAir (the then current titling of what had been and, for that matter, would be again) Canadian Pacific Airlines. To the right is one of the airline's long-haul DC-8-63 models, and in the foreground its DC-8-55F convertible freighter, CF-CPT. Originally built for US operator Panagra in 1966, it entered the CP fleet in November 1967.

Below: After my return to JFK from Montreal on April 19, I saw Braniff's DC-8-62, N1804, now in its two-tone blue "Flying Colors" livery. This aircraft had been ordered by Panagra but was delivered after Braniff had acquired and merged with PG in 1967.

Above: Air France's JT4-powered 707-328, F-BHSS, is ready to depart JFK on April 21, 1974, as seen from the Pan Am Worldport rooftop parking area.

Below: In the early 1970s, the advent of the 747 introduced significant over-capacity in many markets, and some of the smaller carriers that had ordered them were having difficulty in achieving economic travel levels. At this point, Boeing resurrected the "Combi" idea, and converted a pair of 747-100s for Belgium's SABENA, as seen at JFK on April 21, 1974. An advantage of the 747 versus the 707s and DC-8s earlier used for this type of service was the new airplane's ability to accommodate pallets and containers of greater size than the earlier, narrow-body equipment.

Above: Pan Am's *Jet Clipper Yankee* is departing the Worldport on April 21, 1974. Alongside is a smattering of equipment from other carriers at JFK's IAB. The only widebody visible is a TWA 747.

Below: Air France's F-BPVP, a 747-128, appears to be on its way into the gate that F-BHSS (see p. 87) had departed from previously on April 21.

Above: Inbound from Warsaw, Poland is LOT Polish Airlines' IL-62, SP-LAA, at JFK on April 21, 1974.

Below: During the early 1970s, Piedmont, along with many other local service carriers, had expanded considerably, including into markets that had previously been served exclusively by larger/trunk airlines, one example being LGA-ORF (Norfolk, Virginia). In this dramatically lit portrait taken at LGA on April 27, 1974, the *Tarheel Flag Carrier* ("tarheel" being a nickname for North Carolinians) continued to share gate space with Eastern's operations there.

Above: In the spring of 1974, my wife and I embarked on a round-the-world vacation all on TWA, with the exception of the intra-Hawaii flight segments. Our first destination was Bangkok, Thailand, twenty-six hours and two overnights aloft from JFK. Getting to BKK involved a 747 to Rome, followed by a 707-331B that stopped in Tel Aviv and what was then called Bombay, in western India. Departing Bangkok a few days later for Hong Kong allowed some photography on the morning of May 15, including this SAS (Scandinavian Airline Systems) DC-8-62, registered in Norway as LN-MOW.

Opposite above: I also encountered this DC-8-63CF, N8636, which was delivered to Seaboard World Airlines in 1969 and then leased by Korean Air Lines between December 1972 and April 1976.

Opposite below: Finally, on the day of departure from Bangkok, this photo opportunity appeared, parked between our outbound TWA 707 (N873C) and the previously-seen SAS DC-8, in the form of Union of Burma Airways' 727-193. Originally ordered by Pacific Air Lines, it was merged into Air West and then acquired by UBA in July 1970. In 1976 it went to Dan-Air London in the UK. Some surprises can be very good!

KOREAN AIR LINES
대한항공

ပြည်ထောင်စုမြန်မာနိုင်ငံလေကြောင်း
UBA
XY-ADR
SAS

Above: Next stop: Hong Kong's Kai Tak Airport, including the famous "Checkerboard Approach" to runway 13. I noticed on final approach that we were flying between two sets of buildings that were both higher than our altitude at that point, something that did not seem in the least disturbing to the basketball game going on below. On the day we left the then British Crown colony, there was a reasonable amount of time for some photography. Cathay Pacific was the local carrier and, between the demise of its Lockheed Electras and the acquisition of twelve 707-351B/Cs from Northwest Orient beginning in 1971, had been "All Convair 880, All the Time." By May 18, 1974, the 880s were all but gone, and I was happy to get this shot of VH-HGG about to depart, even with the "clutter" in the foreground. I suspect that a US OHSA (Occupational Health and Safety Administration) inspector would not have been happy with the bamboo scaffolding, among other things.

Opposite above: Compared with the traffic volumes that would be achieved within a decade, the Kai Tak that I viewed in 1974 was a sleepy backwater. During my observations, there was only a single widebody present (a Pan Am 747 that would go back to Tokyo after overnighting in HKG). There were carriers present that I had never viewed, however, including this Singapore Airlines 707-312B, which had been delivered to the previous Malaysia-Singapore Airlines in 1968 before the two countries had split their airline operations.

Opposite below: This China Airlines 707-309C, B-1824, seen on short final for runway 13, was delivered to the Taiwan carrier in 1969, and served it until 1982. In 1974, a local English-language newspaper published the Kai Tak arrivals on a daily basis. Though it occupied only part of a single column, pre-internet it was a great way to find out what was coming.

SINGAPORE AIRLINES

CHINA AIRLINES

Above: HS-VGC was a TWA veteran, as N736TW, one of the 707-131 "Water Wagons." The US carrier sold it to Israeli Aircraft Industries in December 1971, which then leased it to Air Siam between September 1973 and March 1975.

Opposite above: In 1974 VR-HGU was representative of what was then Cathay Pacific's *Heavy Iron*, a 707-351C acquired from Northwest Orient in 1973.

Opposite below: After crossing the International Date Line between Guam and Honolulu, it was May 20 when I had the opportunity to photograph at HNL again. Western had dabbled with the early 707s, including hosting a pair of -100 series that had been destined for Cubana Airlines until the US-Cuba political relationship soured in the early 1960s and, after that, chose to concentrate on the smaller 720B with its longer-range capacity. Following the addition of new route authority to Hawaii in the late 1960s, the airline acquired a five-strong fleet of 707-347Cs, one of which, N1505W, is being towed into its gate on one of HNL's marvelous open-air concourses.

VR-HGU
CATHAY PACIFIC

Western
Western

Above: Also on May 20 was this visitor from "down under," in this case New Zealand. In the mid-1970s, a Hawaii stop was mandatory between Australia/New Zealand and the US mainland, and today it is ZK-NZN's turn. At the time of the photo, this aircraft had been in service less than five months; further evidence is provided by the shiny bare metal on the bottom of the fuselage.

Below: *Jet Clipper Eagle* is a 707-321CF, and judging by the windowless fuselage and the wide-open main deck cargo door, N462PA is clearly operating here as a freighter.

Above: On our previous visit to HNL in 1973, I saw this Western 720-047B, N4162, in WA's "traditional" livery. Now in May 1974, it is wearing the airline's new bold graphics, with a switch from maroon to red in the process.

Below: The color red is also prominent in this shot of TWA's 747-131 N93107 at Madrid's Barajas International Airport on August 18, 1974. MAD is at an elevation of about 2,190 feet, making it a "hot and high" location in terms aircraft performance. I recall that takeoff that day on the return trip to JFK required a ground roll of more than sixty seconds before becoming airborne.

Above: Also seen at Barajas on August 18 was Aviaco's Caravelle 10R, EC-BIF. The airline provided service in leisure-oriented Spanish markets to supplement Spain's flag carrier, Iberia. This aircraft had served previously with Iberia and came into the Aviaco fleet in May 1972.

Opposite above: A fall (October 26, 1974) visit to London's Gatwick Airport found this former BOAC 707-436, G-APFD, now operating in inclusive-tour service and based at LGW. From an aircraft enthusiast perspective there was a downside to this, as these aircraft replaced the Comet 4B aircraft that previously had been operating for BEA Airtours.

Opposite below: After shooting at Gatwick in the morning, I returned to Heathrow via the LGW-LHR bus, in preparation for catching TWA's late-afternoon flight 701 back to JFK. Prior to checking in, I spent a modest amount of time at the Queens Building's "spectator" facilities and caught this Balkan Airways IL-18 turboprop, LZ-BEK. Since it was similar in planform, propulsion, and capacity, it was sometimes referred to as the "Russian Electra." In the background we get a good look at Heathrow's cargo facilities, including several "Merchantman" cargo conversions of former BEA Vanguard turboprops, as well as 707 freighters of Pan Am and Brazilian carrier Varig.

British airtours
G-APFO
14

LZ-BEK

Chapter 7

1975

If you choose to go to Canada in late winter—specifically Toronto International Airport (YYZ), in Ontario, on March 10, 1975—it probably should not come as a surprise if there is snow on the ground. The dominant carriers were, of course, Air Canada and CP Air, but there were also a number of "second-level" scheduled passenger carriers that catered to smaller markets in relatively confined geographic areas, somewhat akin to the local service carriers in the US. However, these entities, in many cases, also participated in relatively long-haul leisure-oriented charter services. This photo includes Wardair's 707 C-FPYZ, which tended to focus more on the latter, as well as Manitoba-based Transair.

Above: Here is a closer look at Transair's 737-200, C-GTAR, as it passes my perch on Terminal One's rooftop parking area.

Below: In a nod to Air Canada's significant association with Douglas commercial aircraft types in the early jet age, this view includes a pair of "stretched" DC-8s, a -61 (CF-TJT) in the foreground, and to the rear, a DC-8-63, with a DC-9-30 between the two four-engine types.

Above: BWIA's 9Y-TDR is a truly rare aircraft type, a Boeing 707-227. Only five were built, and only four entered service; the fifth was lost in an accident on a customer acceptance flight prior to delivery. Braniff was the only customer, and what differentiated the -200 from the -100, which was the same size, were the more powerful JT4A engines used on the -200 compared with the JT3C engines in the early -100s, prior to the advent of the fan-powered JT3Ds that would be used in subsequent 707 production. While BWIA (colloquially known as "Bee-Wee") formally stands for "British West Indian Airways," wags preferred "British Worst Investment Abroad."

Below: CP Air's orange-and-bare-metal 747-217B has joined the pack of Air Canada aircraft headed for departure on March 10. C-FCRA is named *Empress of Japan*, reflecting both what was probably the airline's most important market at this point, as well as the multi-modal operations of the Canadian Pacific, whose steamships also bore imperial names.

Above: In this photo we get a good view of both Wardair's 747-127 (later converted to -1D1) and Air Canada's (and its associates') extensive Terminal Two facilities at YYZ. C-FDJC had been intended as N602BN for Braniff, the second of the pair of -100s ordered by the Dallas-based airline. By the time of expected delivery, BN had concluded that a single 747 was all that they needed to service the Dallas-Honolulu route, so this aircraft ended up catering to long-haul holidaymakers for Wardair, as opposed to regional services in western Canada.

Below: Prior to the development of the livery seen on DC-9-30, N1335U, at Washington Dulles International Airport on March 23, 1975, Southern Airways utilized a white fuselage with yellow-and-blue accents that probably could be described as the intersection of traditional and bland. As seen here, the new design was striking by comparison. Unfortunately, this aircraft was lost on April 4, 1977, after losing thrust in both engines in conjunction with a severe thunderstorm. While this event occasioned a considerable loss of life, there were some survivors, including the flight attendants.

Above: Although I had seen and photographed one of BOAC's 707-400s at Gatwick the previous fall, in secondary/package tour service, some of these veteran aircraft continued in first-line scheduled service with British Airways, an example being G-APFJ, operating BA's morning departure from JFK to London on March 11, 1975.

Opposite above: The combination of bright red fuselage and bold graphics seen on Avianca's 720B-030B was a startling change in appearance compared with the carrier's previous conservative blue-on-white livery. As HK-677 was originally with Lufthansa, and later Pan American, it is not unlikely that it had visited JFK multiple times in its previous "lives" before this sighting on May 11, 1975.

Opposite below: By May 1975, TWA was making extensive use of the L-1011 widebodies that it had ordered, including numerous transcontinental routings in the US market. N11005 is seen here taxiing to the west for takeoff on JFK's 14,572ft. runway 13R, as a New York Airways helicopter descends to land.

Avianca Colombia
HK-677
AV

TWA
TWA

Above: N535PA, a 747-273C being operated here as a freighter, was delivered to World Airways in 1973 and leased to Pan Am in 1974, where it became the *Clipper Mercury*. Here, it is seen departing from the pavement of JFK runway 13R on May 11, 1975. Check out the upward deflection of the wing as it becomes airborne!

Opposite above: Piedmont's YS-11A, N187P, (aka *Long Island Pacemaker*) is at Friendship International Airport, in Baltimore, Maryland. Following the "deregulation" of the US domestic market in 1978, Piedmont would eventually establish a hub operation at what then was denoted as BAL. However, on May 14, 1975, this point was essentially an appendage on PI's route system. This is the airline's sole daily departure, operating from and to Washington National Airport (DCA), where it made extensive connections with the rest of Piedmont's route structure at the time.

Opposite below: Small airplanes, but significant portents for the future. This pair of Beech 99s at BAL on May 14, 1975, operated by Henson Aviation and titled *Allegheny Commuter*, were one of the first successful "suspension/replacement" agreements between certificated airlines (trunks and local service) and what were then air-taxi operators to improve service in small markets that were no longer efficient for the larger carriers to serve. In this case, AL had been operating one F-27 (thirty-six-seat) aircraft per day in the Baltimore-Washington, DC (via National Airport) market. Henson replaced this with five weekday flights, and two daily on the weekends, initially with Beech Queen Airs and later the Beech 99s seen here. Ultimately, this would lead to today's "Code Sharing," now utilizing jets with fifty or more seats typically.

PIEDMONT
N187P
PIEDMONT

ALLEGHENY COMMUTER
B99
N596HA

Above: Surprisingly, as its 1960s route structure did not get further away from the "lower 48" US states than Acapulco, Mexico, American signed up for sixteen 747-100s. In contrast, TWA, with a substantial transatlantic operation ordered nineteen. AA concluded fairly quickly that Boeing's new behemoth was not a great fit with their passenger operation and began converting some of their 747s to SCD (side-cargo-door) freighter versions. In addition to using these aircraft for their own all-cargo services, N9676 (seen here departing JFK runway 31L on July 4, 1975) was leased to Lebanon's TMA (Trans Mediterranean Airways). It went on to have a long career as a freighter, eventually working for UPS (United Parcel Service) between 1990 and 2008. In any case, there is a lot of green paint in this view!

Opposite above: While the Cold War would not be effectively over until the early 1990s, it was not unusual to see Russian airliners from Warsaw Pact countries at JFK during the 1970s, including the example here, CSA's *OKjet* IL-62 OK-EBJ on July 4, 1975.

Opposite below: Taxiing east, parallel to 13R/13L, is El Al's 707-358C, 4X-ATY, delivered to the Israeli carrier in 1970. It appears to be in all-cargo service.

OK JET
OK-EBG
FLAMMABLE
650

EL AL

Above: With the upcoming celebration of the US Bicentennial in 1976, several airlines made an effort to commemorate this event. One such airline was Eastern, in the form of a colorful sticker on the forward fuselage of its L-1011, N308A, exactly a year before the anniversary. Seen here at JFK on July 4, 1975, it taxies by the Pan Am Worldport.

Below: Air Afrique's DC-8-53, TU-TCB, seen here at JFK on July 26, 1975, was delivered to the multi-national African carrier in January 1964. Here it is in the process of departing the IAB ramp and shortly will be "taking care of [the] business" of the airline's weekly nonstop flight from New York to Dakar, Senegal, and points beyond.

Above: After the Air Afrique departure was the arrival of VT-EBE, Air India's 747-237 *Emperor Shahjehan*, the airline's second 747, delivered in April 1971, complete with the carrier's signature livery feature of pointed window trim.

Below: Following the Air India 747 to the IAB to discharge its passengers on July 26, 1975, was Varig's 707-324C, PP-VLL. The Brazilian airline acquired this long-haul narrow-body in April 1972 from its original owner, Continental. It would stay in the Varig fleet until 1987.

After the arrival of the Indian Emperor, there was a Nordic departure, in the form of Danish-registered (OY-KHA) 747, SAS's *Ivar Viking*. The scene recorded here, featuring airlines from two different continents at a third continental location (North America)—in effect, half of the world's historically inhabited continents—speaks much about the global imprint of the 747, even by the mid-1970s.

In terms of aircraft size, things were definitely on a smaller scale at La Guardia on August 12, 1975. Though there is also variety here, it is limited to airlines of a single country, namely the US. Five different airlines are visible, along with six different liveries. As this was my first experience photographing Allegheny's "new" paint scheme on N979VJ, with the previous version on N940VJ in the foreground, I do not know that if this livery change had a name, but it quickly acquired one: "Three Streaks of Rust," referencing AL's Pittsburgh hub and principal maintenance facility, located in what was becoming known as the US's "Rust Belt."

Above: By October 2, 1975, local service carrier Ozark was becoming a growing presence at Lambert Field Airport in St. Louis, Missouri. This DC-9-30, N984Z, was OZ's top-of-the-line equipment then, as the carrier provided services that increasingly competed with TWA, historically the largest carrier at STL.

Below: As seen here, at Nashville, Tennessee on October 8, 1975, Southern Airways was still operating piston-powered aircraft, in this case, former Eastern Airlines Martin 404s, including N141. In fact, SO, which once used the term "Aristocrats" to describe the type, would be the last of the Local Service carriers to use piston aircraft, on April 30, 1978.

Above: By 1975, a number of Martin 404s had filtered down to smaller carriers, including N40425, now with Southeast Airlines, at Miami International on November 4, 1975. This aircraft was delivered to TWA in June 1952 and would go to Piedmont between 1965 and 1968, followed by a succession of other smaller operators, until being destroyed by a hurricane in 1989.

Opposite above: Also seen at Miami in November 1975 was Lanica's Convair 880, AN-BIA. Originally destined to be N829TW, it flew with Northeast Airlines between 1962 and 1967, when it was supplanted by that carrier's new 727-200s. It later served with the Nicaraguan carrier between July 1972 and February 1975, following which it was stored, as seen here.

Opposite below: Air Florida's L-188 Lockheed Electra N25AF began its career with Northwest Orient Airlines in 1959 and was with the trunk carrier until 1971. It joined the upstart, then intrastate airline Air Florida in August 1974 and was there until July 1977. Air Florida would expand considerably beyond its initial service with a single Boeing 707 and eventually operate widebody aircraft on international routes.

N25AF
AIR FLORIDA

Above: This Curtis-Wright C-46A *Commando* came into service (literally, with the US army air forces) in the closing months of World War II, in June 1945. I photographed it at MIA on November 4, 1975, during its stint with Bahamasair. Its "double-bubble" fuselage created lots of cubic capacity, which made it a popular vehicle for hauling cargo.

Opposite above: A month after these shots at Miami International, on December 12, 1975, I was in a considerably cooler climate and shot this TWA "C-jet" N5773T on a daytime layover at Boston's Logan International Airport. This involved transcontinental flights to the west coast of the US during the hours of darkness, especially at this time of the year. The company's hangar at BOS is behind the aircraft, in case the signage was not conspicuous enough.

Opposite below: Over on the passenger side of Logan the same day, TWA's 707-331B, N8702, is undergoing turnaround servicing, with an FH-227C and Aero Commander 500B of Air New England between me and the TWA aircraft. N374NE might seem familiar, and yes, this aircraft did begin its career with Northeast Airlines in 1966 and passed into Delta at the time of that carrier's acquisition of Northeast in 1972. DL ended up finding that short-haul routes with turboprops in New England were no more lucrative than they had been for Northeast. As a result, these aircraft and the routes they served were transferred in 1974 to Air New England, a former air taxi company, when it became the first "new" airline to be certificated by the US CAB (Civil Aeronautics Board) since the creation of the local service carriers post-World War II. In effect this re-created a portion of the original Northeast, prior to its addition of routes to Florida. Yes, the more things change, sometimes they not only remain the same, but revert to previous times...

TWA
CARGOJET
N5773T
T W A
TWA

TWA
Air
NewEngland
274NE
N6106X

Chapter 8

1976

Above: On the cold and windy morning of January 29, 1976, this was my ride: TWA flight 614's convenient 0430 (4:30 AM in "civilian" parlance) freighter departure from Los Angeles to St. Louis via Kansas City, utilizing its 707-331C, N15711. Since freighters could depart ahead of schedule once all the cargo was on board, actual departure from LAX that morning was 0413.

Opposite above: Most of the traffic on this flight was a shipment of CB (Citizens Band) radios (cell phones were still a long way off) from Asia to a US distributor in the Kansas City area. An Igloo (a type "A" container) is seen here during the unloading process, with others awaiting their ride to the ramp are still onboard the aircraft under the wide-open main-deck cargo door.

Opposite below: Since there was little or no cargo that needed to be loaded for the relatively short second segment of flight 614 to STL, the cockpit crew was beginning preparations for returning N15711 to the air. My recollection is that we arrived at Lambert Field about forty-five minutes ahead of schedule.

CARGOJET
TWA

Above: An industry cargo meeting in San Juan, Puerto Rico took me "offline" TWA's route system on April 29, 1976. At SJU, I watched the departure of Iberia's DC-10-30, EC-CSJ.

Below: Far more prolific at Luis Muñoz Marin International Airport than Iberia aircraft were the DeHavilland DH-114 Herons utilized by what was essentially an air taxi operation between Ponce, Puerto Rico, and San Juan operated by Prinair. The four-engine piston aircraft featured a livery that utilized different colors on individual aircraft using the same design: in effect a "mini-Braniff" approach.

Above: Delta was another carrier that honored the US Bicentennial year of 1976, in this case, by creating a "stars and stripes" version of the Delta "widget," as seen here on N3333L at ATL on August 11, 1976. Interestingly, I had ridden this aircraft to ATL for an interview with Delta in the fall of 1971, during my graduate student days.

Below: On the same afternoon, I also observed Piedmont's approach to celebrating 200 years of US independence via the use of a sticker on the forward fuselage, similar to Eastern's approach. With N759N (a former United Airlines aircraft acquired by PI in March 1976), they took this to a different level, however, naming it the *Bicentennial Pacemaker*.

Above: Also at ATL on August 11 was a 737-222 still in United's employ, N9022U, the *City of Grand Rapids*. This "four-star" evolution of United's paint scheme was referred to as the "Circus" paint scheme in some quarters.

Opposite above: While this might appear to be an airport where United was prominent, that "Fly Delta Jets" sign on the maintenance facility in the background is a clear indication that we are in the city where Delta is headquartered. In reality this is a photograph of the remnant of the former Capital Airlines route structure which United had acquired in June 1961 under the "failing business" doctrine, where regulated businesses like airlines were not permitted to fail. And yes, Capital met the "failing" test conclusively at that point.

Opposite below: A quick trip had me in London on September 8, 1976, and provided my first opportunity to photograph a Concorde in scheduled service, as G-BOAA exited the Terminal Three ramp on September 8. By the way, I am standing next to a Wookey (not to be confused with a Wookiee). If you worked for TWA in the 1970s and 80s, or Northwest in the 90s, you may recognize the reference.

FLY DELTA JETS
United
UNITED
YIELD

British airways

Above: Later that afternoon, as I was about to board TWA flight 701 for JFK, I saw this interesting combination of carrier and livery: G-APFB, one of the initial BOAC 707-436s, still soldiering on a decade and a half after first use, although now wearing British Airtours branding. The color scheme it was wearing likely stemmed from its lease to Syrian Arab Airlines from March 1974 until February 1975.

Below: The final significant operator of the Convair 990 was Spanish inclusive-tour operator Spantax. EC-BJD is at Madrid Barajas on November 10, 1976.

Chapter 9

1977

By early 1977, TWA has adopted a new livery replacing the classic, well-liked "double globe" scheme that dated from early in the jet era. This was the 1970s, and there seemed to be considerable impetus to be "in the moment." The new colors continued to feature red and white prominently, without the previous gold accents. Initially the "Trans World Airline" titles were simply in red outline. This later was changed to solid blocks of red, which stood out considerably better. Here is N5773T, one of the few 707 freighters to have the new look applied, at SFO on January 17, 1977.

Above: While Allegheny had amassed a large fleet of jet aircraft and had begun the process of substituting commuter carriers in its smallest markets, it had considerable use for the twin-turboprop Convair 580s that were still in its fleet, including this pair at New York La Guardia on February 11, 1977. Powered by the same Allison engines used on the Lockheed L-188 Electra, they were well liked for their ample power. One description of the 580 was "half an Electra." Certain people familiar with their operation might have lobbied for 60 percent instead.

Opposite above: It is relatively unusual to see aircraft that are leased from another carrier in service with the name of both airlines in view. In this case it was United's 737-222, N9029U, the *City of Lansing*, which was leased to intra-Hawaii carrier Aloha between June 1976 and September 1977. Aloha's regular 737 livery can be seen at the right. Both aircraft are at Kahalui, Maui, on March 14, 1977.

Opposite below: Back in Honolulu on the same day, here is a look at Aloha's intrastate rival, Hawaiian Air. Their twin-jet preference was the McDonnell Douglas DC-9, three of which can be seen here.

United
N9029U
737 Friend Ship
Aloha
SHEL

HAWAIIAN AIR
HAWAIIAN AIR
HAWA

Above: A short distance to the east, considerably "heavier" metal was the order of the day, as United's long-haul DC-8-62, N8969U, now in the livery designed by Saul Bass. It is essentially surrounded by jumbos, in the form of a pair of United 747s, along with Wardair Canada's contribution of the same type.

Opposite above: Even before deregulation, some of the gate concourses at LGA featured colorful displays of aircraft, including the one seen here on April 6, 1977, which included four airlines, five liveries and three aircraft types.

Opposite below: On June 12, 1977, Varig's DC-10-30s have supplanted the 707s used by the Brazilian carrier for its New York route. PP-VMD is on display coming by the Pan Am Worldport.

ALLEGHENY
BRANIFF INTERNATIONAL
BI
Flying Colors
Southern
United

VARIG
DC-10
PP-VMD
VARIG
BRASIL
AA

Above: Not far behind the Varig "Ten" was this Pan Am 747 freighter, N771PA, bearing the name *Donald McKay*. Delivered as a passenger airplane in August 1970, it was converted to a "side door" cargo configuration in March 1975.

Opposite above: On June 21, 1977, here is what Southern Airways' crowded ramp at ATL looked like. A pair of Martin 404s retain their traditional colors, while the three DC-9s present are in the newer blue-and-white livery.

Opposite below: DC-9s were also in evidence at the Atlanta concourse serving both Eastern and Piedmont, with four of the Douglas designs in Eastern's two-tone "Hockey Stick" colors were bracketed by a pair of Piedmont aircraft: a YS-11A, in its as-delivered livery, while the 727-100 at the far end is in the airline's more recent colors, featuring a paler shade of blue. The latter is without the striping included in the "classic" Piedmont paint scheme, which dated all the way back to the carrier's use of the DC-3.

Southern
Southern
SOUTHERN
SOUTHERN

PIEDMONT
EASTERN
EASTERN
EASTERN
N8977E
Whisperjet

Above: Seen here are a widebody, in the form of Avianca's 747-124F HK-2000, and a narrow-body, Air France's Supersonic Concorde F-BVFD at Paris-Charles de Gaulle on July 13, 1977. Surprisingly, the latter is only about 20ft. shorter than the 747, even though its seat capacity is about one-fourth of the Boeing product. And the Concorde as a "narrow-body"? Its cabin cross section was similar to that of the DC-9, so why not?

Opposite above: It is the day before the French national holiday Bastille Day, and both national airlines in the Paris-London market are utilizing widebody aircraft in this market: British Airways with L-1011s, and Air France with its then 3-year-old A300B2, F-BVGA, the fifth production aircraft of this type, and the first delivery to Air France.

Opposite below: Here, *Gulf Alpha* is pulling away from the gate on its way to London Heathrow. Often when you travel you learn things that would have been helpful to have known about in advance, such as the wisdom in avoiding airline pass/non-revenue travel on the day before a major holiday. However, the wait did allow me to watch several hours of CDG-LHR departures before finally getting on F-BVGF. I would have preferred the "extra section" that was operating with a Caravelle in conjunction with this departure, but when you are traveling standby and they give you a boarding pass, it is wise to go ahead and use it!

British airways
A300B2
107

AIR FRANCE
F-BVGA
GA

Above: Business completed the next day in England, there was time for some plane watching and photography at Heathrow before heading home. This colorful Vickers VC-10 was "ready for her close-up," and I was happy to have the opportunity. Built for and utilized initially by BOAC, the livery and *Gulf Air* title reflected the fact that *Victor Juliet* was leased by the government of Qatar between October 1975 and April 1981.

Below: Here is a look at a pair of tri-jets at LHR on July 14, 1977, neither of which is a Boeing 727. In the foreground is Hungarian Airline Malev's HA-LCH, also referred to as the "Russian 727" on occasion. In the far background is a British-built Hawker-Siddeley Trident, which appears to be in Cyprus Airways livery.

Above: Another visit to LHR on August 24, 1977, provided the opportunity to tour the airport's cargo facilities. Present during my visit was Seaboard World's 747 "Containership," N702SW. One of the airline's purpose-built containers can be seen emerging from the aircraft's nose. Check out the size of the tail jack needed for this behemoth!

Below: Nearby the ramp where the Seaboard 747 was unloading, this British Airways 707-336C freighter was also being attended to, at what was referred to as the airline's "freight shed."

Above: Olympic's YS-11A, SX-BBH, awaits the passengers for its morning flight from the island of Mykonos, Greece to the capital, Athens, on October 27, 1977. The Greek flag carrier operated the Japanese airframe / Rolls Royce-powered twin turboprops on domestic services, including island-hopping routes to Greek islands in the Aegean Sea. The airport at Mykonos has a 6,200ft. runway, with sharp drop-offs at both ends, making arrivals and departures here, from a passenger perspective, relatively dramatic.

Below: Back at ATH on October 29, heavier metal was again in view, including the US "supplemental" carrier Capitol's DC-8-61, N912CL. Even more interesting was the Dan-Air Comet 4C in the foreground. The British-built Comet was, of course, the "jet that started it all," with the Comet 1 entering commercial airline service in 1952, well in advance of the Boeing 707, Douglas DC-8, or even the Soviet TU-104. By this time, Dan-Air has cornered the market for the type, which it used principally in leisure/inclusive-tour service. At the end of November 1980 this Comet's civil career will be over, however.

Above: Also seen at Athens Hellinikon Airport on October 29 was this UK-registered BAC 111-500, leased by Cyprus Airways between the fall of 1976 and early 1978.

Below: While Yugoslavia was considered a communist nation during the post-World War II Cold War years, it was forced out of the Soviet Union's major alliance, the Warsaw Pact, in 1948. As a result, the Yugoslav national airline was able to make use of "western" aircraft. YU-AGE, a 707-340C, was delivered originally to Pakistan Airlines in July 1966, and then sold to Jugoslovenski Aero Transport in May 1972. Check out the numerous Olympic aircraft across the runway in the distance at ATH, the carrier's base of operations, on October 29, 1978. Notice the belt loader in use at the rear passenger door.

Chapter 10

1978

Above: A pair of ANA (All Nippon Airways) Lockheed L-1011s are on view here at Tokyo's Haneda Airport on Valentine's Day, 1978, with JA8511 at the left. No enclosed boarding bridges are in use here, so the boarding passengers will get a good workout walking up the stairs to their widebody ride.

Opposite above: Pan Am's Boeing 747SP, N534PA, the *Clipper Great Republic*, does offer its passengers an enclosed boarding experience that places boarding passengers at doorway level. Pan Am acquired this "short-body" (i.e., fewer seats and greater range) 747 type specifically for operating its New York-Tokyo nonstop, which it is doing here.

Opposite below: By the late 1970s, Japan's (and much of East Asia's) economy was booming, and this included the air-cargo industry. Here is a view of the cargo facilities at Haneda on February 14, 1978, along with some freighters, as well as passenger aircraft at remote parking positions. If this does not look like the first-class facilities that you would expect at the Japanese capital's airport, there is a reason: virtually all international operations will shift from Haneda to the new Narita Airport several months later, making it clear that updating HND's cargo facilities was not worthwhile.

PAN AM
Clipper Great Republic
42

Above: In the seven years since 1971, when I had seen Cathay's relatively newly-acquired Boeing 707 at Haneda, the carrier had grown considerably. Now, its flagship equipment was the widebody L-1011 TriStar, such as VR-HHL, a -100 model (or, as CX has identified it on the number two engine inlet, a "Super" version), also at Tokyo Haneda on February 14, 1978.

Below: Eastern Airlines was the first carrier to adopt the Airbus A300 twin widebody in the US. The European manufacturer utilized an unusual "try it, you'll like it" deal with the venerable US trunk carrier, where it leased the initial group of four A300s rather than purchasing them outright. This proved to be successful, and Eastern became a significant operator of the type. Here is N202EA at JFK on March 11, 1978. Judging by the lower left corner of the photo, winter in New York City does not appear to be over yet.

Sabena was not the only European airline to utilize 747 Combi aircraft on transatlantic routes. Here, LN-RNA is being serviced at JFK on March 11, 1978. To its right is Swissair's DC-10-30, HB-IHE.

Taxiing by the SAS and Swissair aircraft is Pan Am's 747-121, N731PA, bearing what looks like a sticker informing us that this is, at least for the moment, *Clipper Friendship Force*. The Friendship Force International was an organization promoted by US President Jimmy Carter in the late 1970s that encouraged groups of people from different cultures to exchange home visits with each other. N731PA was delivered as the *Clipper Bostonian* and would adopt the *Clipper Ocean Express* designation in 1980.

Above: Here, at JFK, on March 11, 1978, is another example of a US airline using the Nord 262. N7885A, following service in Europe between 1966 and 1977. Following its use by Altair, it went back to Europe in November 1981. Altair was a Philadelphia-based "commuter" carrier that operated between 1966 and 1982.

Opposite above: Also arriving at JFK on March 11 was Iran Air's 747, EP-IAH, which was nothing out of the ordinary at the time. In November 1979, following the Iranian Revolution, what became known as the Iran hostage crisis occurred, resulting in Iran Air discontinuing service to the US

Opposite below: On the morning of April 1, 1978, Seaboard World's "Containership," N702SW, was taxiing parallel to JFK runway 31L while an Air Jamaica 727-200 was climbing out following takeoff on 13R.

IRAN AIR

SEABOARD WORLD Containership
SW
N702SW

Above: Ten days later, on April 11, 1978, the very first 747 freighter, Lufthansa's D-ABYE, has just become airborne on 13R, also at JFK.

Opposite above: At the Pan Am Worldport at JFK on April 11, 1978, Avianca's HK-2015 is being pushed back for departure. It is no stranger to either the airport or terminal facility, since this 707-321B was Pan Am's *Clipper Bald Eagle* between its delivery in 1967 and the Colombian carrier's acquisition of it in February 1977.

Opposite below: In the spring of 1978, I left the New York City area for Houston, Texas to work for Texas International Airlines; you can expect to see a considerable number of photos taken in the Lone Star State going forward! As an introduction, here is a look at the TI maintenance facility, across the street from the carrier's headquarters at Houston's Hobby Airport in what was known as the "Blue Barn." In addition to the pair of DC-9s in the hangar, I was lucky to capture one of the few remaining Convair 600s in the TI fleet, since by this time, August 23, 1978, these turboprops were used to provide service between Albuquerque and Carlsberg, Clovis, and Hobbs, all located in New Mexico.

AV
Avianca Colombia

Texas International
08

Above: With the exception of Southwest Airlines, most of Houston's airline service in the late 1970s utilized IAH, then known as Intercontinental Airport. This included a fair amount of international service, including both to points in Mexico and Central America as well as longer-haul flights to Europe. The Air France 747 and British Caledonian 707 (a relatively recent addition at the time, August 26, 1978) fit the latter description, while the Pan Am 707 provided service in both the Latin American markets and connected the airline's global route structure. with its hub at JFK.

Opposite above: Presaging the future, this trio of TI DC-9, National 727, and Continental 727 at IAH on October 14, 1978, reflects future possibilities for TI, in terms of its proposed acquisition of National and, several years later, its successful acquisition and merger with Continental.

Opposite below: Even in the late 1970s, the Houston metropolitan area encompassed a great deal of land area and continued to expand in all directions, although it was somewhat constrained by water (Trinity Bay) to the Southeast. There was little if any public transportation in the newly-minted suburbs, which produced significant congestion on the region's freeways, where virtually all commuting involved automobiles. Accordingly, a commuter airline, Metro, was established to provide local-feeder service from the area southeast of the city, in particular to the area around the NASA Johnson Space Center. This airline utilized high-performance (in terms of takeoff and landing runway requirements) DeHavilland Canada DHC-6 "Twin Otter" aircraft and benefitted from the use of specialized STOL (short takeoff and landing) runways at IAH that enabled it to avoid runway congestion there. A pair of the turboprops can be seen at IAH, also on October 14, 1978.

CONTINENTAL
N40483

Texas International
N927MA
N926MA

Above: On the same day, all-cargo carrier Airlift provided N8215U for my camera to capture. This 1960 DC-8-30 was part of Pan Am's original order for the type, as N808PA, *Clipper Gauntlet*, and was acquired by United in 1967. Later, it was converted to a freighter and leased by Airlift, as seen here. Yet even without "United" titles, the "economy" paint scheme leaves little doubt about the aircraft's prior affiliation.

Opposite above: Another interesting freighter seen on October 14 was LV-MSG, of Argentina's TAR (Transporte Aereos Rioplatense). This 707-321C had been delivered to Pan Am in 1963 as *Clipper Challenger* and was acquired by TAR in July 1978, so this was somewhat of a "new kid on the block" from that perspective. To its rear is Pan Am's 747, N744PA, *Clipper Sovereign of the Seas*.

Opposite below: Following these photographs at IAH on October 14, 1978, I headed for New Orleans International Airport, where I found SAHSA's 737-200, HR-SHA, pushed back and ready to depart. To its left was a Braniff 727-100, N309BN, in the two-tone blue "Flying Colors" paint scheme.

PAN AM
N755PA
TAR
CARGO
LV-MSG

BI
Flying Colors
309BN
SAHSA

Above: Also at MSY that day was another aircraft featuring blue coloration, albeit of a darker hue, in the form of Southern Airways' DC-9-15, N94S, delivered from the manufacturer in February 1968.

Below: Back in Houston, I made a specific trip to IAH to see this aircraft on December 4, 1978. Apparently British Caledonian was doing well in the Houston-London passenger market (served via London's Gatwick Airport), and Houston was also a strong cargo market, so BR leased this aircraft from Ireland's Aer Lingus (where it was EI-ASJ, *St. Patrick*) for a portion of the winter 1978/79 season, using the British registration G-BDPZ to provide additional capacity in the market.

Chapter 11

1979

Purely by chance on February 25, 1979, I caught N1038V after it arrived at Houston Intercontinental. This aircraft began its career as Pan American's B-377 Stratocruiser *Clipper Constitution* in September 1949, before Aero Spacelines in 1965 converted it into a 377-SG "Super Guppy," complete with an expanded fuselage to carry outsized cargo.

Above: Following the Super Guppy sighting, I saw this trio of Texas International DC-9s at Terminal A, including a pair of -30s and N1053T, a -14 that TI had acquired from its original owner, TWA, in September 1977.

Opposite above: A somewhat slower form of air cargo transport was at IAH on February 25, 1979, in the form of Costa Rican airline Exaco's DC-6A freighter, TI-ALS. Built originally for Aramco in Saudi Arabia (the Arab American Oil Company) in 1956, it was sold to LACSA in Costa Rica in 1960. By the late 1970s, seeing a classic-era "Large Prop" at a major US airport was relatively uncommon, and I was glad to have the opportunity.

Opposite below: A recent scheduled-service addition at IAH as of February 25 was Cayman Airways, providing nonstop service between Houston and Grand Cayman. Doing the honors here is VR-CAL, a 1970 BAC 111-500 that served several other carriers before arriving at Cayman in May 1978.

EX
TI-ALS
EXACO cargo

Cayman Airways
VR-CAL

Above: Caravelles were not a common sight in the US. Only United acquired the type new, and, while both Air France and Brazil's Varig used the type on services from the Caribbean and Latin America, respectively, the thought of a US operator with a Caravelle freighter would have been viewed as ludicrous a few years before this February 25, 1979, photo at IAH. Cargo deregulation in the US started in 1977 (about a year before the passenger version), and this created a demand for smaller narrow-body freighters, preferably inexpensive ones. Thus, we have Midwest Air Charter, operating for Airborne using N904MW, a Series-VIR, originally United's N1008U, the *Ville de Rochefort*. A far cry from the days of United's premium "Executive" service!

Opposite above: April 8, 1979, brought this exotic creature to IAH: a Canadair CL-44D4 turboprop based on the Bristol Britannia. The "D4" in the designation indicates that this version has a "swing tail," as can be readily seen here. This feature made it easier to load lengthy pieces of cargo. At the crew's invitation, I was able to board the aircraft and view the cockpit and galley area. The latter contained what was clearly a household/consumer-grade toaster oven, which appeared to be the device used to provide hot (or maybe warm) food on board. About two years after this photo, this aircraft was lost in mid-air collision with a Su-15 fighter from the Soviet Union near Yerevan, in present-day Armenia.

Opposite below: While Pan American initially ordered more DC-8s than 707s, Boeing company products, primarily the two seen here on April 15, 1979, the 707 and 747, were the mainstays of the airline's fleet during the jet age. That is *Clipper Queen of the Sky* to the left, while *Clipper Jupiter* towers over the earlier type.

TRANSPORTE AEREO RIOPLATENSE

PAN AM
PAN AM

Above: A trip to eastern Canada in June 1979, in conjunction with TI's application to serve Montreal and Toronto, provided the opportunity to see Quebecair's 707-123B, C-GQBG, at the latter's international airport on June 9, 1979. As mentioned earlier in conjunction with this location, Canada's "regional" airlines also operated longer-haul services catering to leisure passenger markets, so it is likely that *Quebec Bravo Golf* (sounds like an advertising slogan for the province!) is being utilized in that role here.

Opposite above: On June 30, 1979, this freighter visited IAH. As you might suspect, given the N791TW registration, this 707-331C, built in 1964, was operated until March 1979 by TWA, primarily as a freighter, although TWA's all-cargo service officially ended on December 31, 1978. Global International was founded in 1978, in Kansas City, Missouri, once also the headquarters of TWA, and not until 1981 did it operate passenger flights.

Opposite below: By June 30,1979, Braniff had begun to implement a third iteration of its colorful approach to airline liveries, in the form of the "Ultra" colors seen on the pair of blue 727s bracketing the -100 (N7284). The -100 is still in the phase-two "Flying Colors" introduced in the early 1970s, which featured four sets of two-tone color combinations. Deregulation is now picking up speed, as is evident from the presence of the Allegheny 727, used to provide service to IAH from AL's Pittsburgh hub.

GIA
ORAS GLOBAL INTERNATIONAL AIRWAYS
N791TW

BI
Flying Colors
BI
BI
Braniff
26

Above: While National Airlines did not have a full-scale hub at Houston, they did have several "mini connecting complexes" over the course of a given day on their Florida-West Coast routes. This group of three NA 727-200s, complete with bold "Sun King" graphics on their tails, is engaging in this process.

Opposite above: Even at the dawn of the 747 era nine years earlier, who would have predicted that a Jordanian airliner would have the type in its fleet, and would serve Houston Intercontinental with it? Well, here is the indisputable evidence: JY-AFB, a Combi, taxies by Terminal A at IAH on June 30, 1979.

Opposite below: South of downtown Houston, on the hot, humid morning of August 13, 1979, this photo indicates that deregulation has been good to Hobby Airport, as well as IAH, both via the expansion of Southwest Airlines, the primary user of that facility, as well as the addition of HOU to the route structure of other carriers, including what is now known as Hughes Air West.

alia
elle
THE ROYAL JORDANIAN AIRLINE
PRINCESS HAYA

Above: Back at IAH on September 3, 1979, we see that following the carrier's usage of the 747 in late 1978 and early 1979, British Caledonian is now operating the DC-10-30 on its London-Houston route, a more appropriately sized vehicle. Notice the "Lion Rampant" on G-BEBL's tail. BR used the tag line "Take a Lion to London" in its local advertising in Houston during this period.

Opposite above: This Airlift DC-8 freighter (a Series 54) has the carrier's full paint scheme, as opposed to the "hybrid" United colors seen earlier. On September 3, 1979, it is seen together with an Allegheny 727 arriving from Pittsburgh. This particular DC-8 and sister ship N109RD were leased to National Airlines when it was awarded a nonstop route from Miami to London in 1970, since National's own DC-8s lacked the range needed for this route. When this proved to be a success, NA replaced the leased Airlift aircraft with its own 747s.

Opposite below: Re-branding in process at Boston Logan on September 16, 1979 as "Allegheny" becomes USAir. As the once-local service carrier expanded outside its historic service territory as a result of deregulation, the airline's management felt that they needed a name that indicated the new geographic reach. Notice that the loading bridges have yet to have their nomenclature updated. In any case, the "Three Streaks of Rust" livery on N953VJ has survived the change.

AIRLIFT
AIRLIFT
N108RD

4
6
ALLEGHENY
USAIR

Above: Aeroflot's IL-62M, CCCP-86485, is ready to taxi from Pan Am's Worldport as it prepares to depart JFK on September 19, 1979. Notice the sticker on the fuselage identifying the airline as the "Official Olympic Carrier," a reference to the then upcoming 1980 Summer Olympics in Moscow. Due to the Soviet Union's invasion of Afghanistan, President Jimmy Carter will have the US boycott the games, ultimately rendering the marketing seen here of little or no value.

Opposite above: A visit to Miami, Florida on September 25, 1979, indicates that startup airline Air Florida has moved beyond the turboprop Lockheed Electra that we saw earlier. Its DC-9-15RC (*Rapid Change*, reflecting both passenger and cargo capabilities), N50AF, began its airline career with Continental in April 1967 and would also be utilized by Air Canada before joining the Sunshine State carrier in June 1978, a little over a year prior to this photo.

Opposite below: Back at Houston Intercontinental on September 30, 1979, I encountered an aircraft relatively new to Braniff: a 727-30C, N311BN. While the airline was adding significant numbers of new 727-200s to its fleet, its apparent need for even more capacity caused them to source this -100, originally built for Germany's Lufthansa, three months before the current date, in June 1979. Since the "Ultra" colors were now standard, N311BN received the "Chocolate Brown" version of the livery, one of only a small number of the carrier's 727-100s to wear the "latest and greatest."

air florida
N50AF

Braniff
N311BN

Above: Here, N311BN has arrived at a gate where it is the centerpiece of "Ultra" colors, including a pair of 727-200s: N459BN in Light Blue, and N456BN in Perseus Green.

Opposite above: Later in the week, a trip to England afforded the opportunity to visit Gatwick on October 4, 1979. Remaining on the colorful Braniff theme, here is a "Big Orange" 747 of the Texan carrier heading into its gate that morning. This one was a 747-273C convertible version, here in all-passenger configuration, leased from World Airways, as indicated by its registration, N749WA.

Opposite below: Over at Heathrow the next day, October 5, is a local UK product, a Hawker-Siddeley Trident 3B, G-AWYZ. To get better takeoff performance for this "stretched" model, a booster engine was installed above the "regular" number two powerplant, to be used as needed. Wags took to calling this model the "best four-engine tri-jet extant."

BRANIFF INTERNATIONAL
British airtours

British airways
Trident three
G-AWYZ
Mobil

Above: No prizes for guessing the location of this photo, which also has considerable British commercial aerospace content, in the form of two Tridents and a Lockheed L-1011, G-BBAG, powered by British-built Rolls-Royce RB211 engines.

Opposite above: Following the steep rise in the price of oil and its derivative products beginning in 1973, traffic to and from the Middle East burgeoned. One of the beneficiaries of this was Kuwait Airways, which, during the early part of the decade, had a modest fleet of Boeing 320Cs. By late in the decade, additional 707s were added, along with 747-200 Combis, including 9K-ADC, as seen here on October 5 at LHR.

Opposite below: Over at Heathrow's Terminal Three ramp was this British classic Super VC-10, G-ASGL, one of the most beautiful airliners ever built, in my opinion. Unfortunately, since it (and the original model, the VC-10) was designed to meet BOAC (British Overseas Airways Corporation) specifications, it had excellent performance capabilities, useful on what were called the airline's "Empire Routes," particularly at "hot and high" locations. However, its economics were worse than those of the Boeing 707 and Douglas DC-8, which dominated the market for long-haul aircraft prior to the advent of widebodies.

KUWAIT AIRWAYS
FAIRCLOUGH
Welcome to Britain

British airways
MEA
air BP

Above: Tridents were still numerous at Terminal One, the former home of BEA (British European Airways), but this view also shows an "interloper" in the form of a Boeing 737, which we will see more of later on. All of the aircraft are in the first British Airways paint scheme.

Opposite above: Though not an airplane picture, it was the venue for obtaining many photographs "back in the day." This was the entrance to the "viewing area" located on top of the Queen's Building, between LHR Terminals One and Two. An idea of its popularity can be gained by reading the first paragraph of the sign on the right, which states that only 5,000 people could be accommodated at a time. With the Concorde being in service at the time, the sign to the left of the doorway provides information about its arrival and departure times.

Opposite below: As of October 20, 1979, I was back in Texas and made a trip to Addison, between Dallas and Fort Worth, to see a particular aircraft type, one with a British connection as well. N80FA is an American/British hybrid that began life as a Douglas piston-engine DC-4 (or its military counterpart, the C-54). The bulbous nose was installed to ferry automobiles across the English Channel, with their owners and passengers riding in the rear of the aircraft. Up to five automobiles could be accommodated at a time. By late 1979, this one was hauling cargo in the US market. The cubic capacity added in the process of converting a DC-4 to was also useful for outsized cargo loads. The person behind this process was none other than Freddie Laker, of the UK, utilizing his firm Aviation Traders (Engineering) Limited to convert DC-4s to ATL-98 Carvairs.

Roof Gardens
Way In
Roof gardens
close to day at 5·00 pm
Dogs are not allowed on Roof gardens.
Tickets available on day of issue only.
to be shown on demand. not transferable
Amusement arcade
Childrens playground
Commentators box
Cafeteria
Shop
Snack bar
The cafeteria closes one hour before the closure of the Roof Gardens but no later than 18 00 hours
Skate boards are not permitted on the Roof Gardens
Owners are advised that they may use the B.A.A. Left Baggage office (opposite Terminal 2) to deposit their property for safe custody prior to entry to the Roof Gardens
There will be a charge for such deposits
The British Airports Authority wishes to advise visitors that under the existing fire regulations the permitted number of people that may be present on the Roof Gardens at any one time must not exceed 5000.
During busy spells it may become necessary to stop admission for a time when the maximum number is reached.
We very much regret any incovenience caused and would ask our visitors to understand that this measure is being taken in the intrests of the health and safety of the public.

AIRWAYS
CARGO
N80FA

Above: So, you believe that Southwest Airlines has only ever operated one type of aircraft, the Boeing 737? Better shut your eyes... WN used Boeing 727s in scheduled service twice. The first iteration, part of the settlement of an anti-trust case won by Southwest against Braniff and Texas International, involved BN providing a 727-200 for use by Southwest. Thus, we see N406BN landing at Love Field in Dallas on December 10, 1979, in full Southwest livery, including script lettering that I do not believe was seen before, or after. Southwest concluded that the 727 did not fit their operation well (being unable to match 737 turnaround times, for example) and returned the aircraft in January 1980.

Opposite above: The deregulation of all-cargo operations in the US beginning in 1977 enabled what was then called Federal Express to make the jump from business jets (Dassault Falcons) to Boeing 727s in a single step. Here is evidence of this at Houston's Hobby Airport on October 25, 1979. N111FE previously was N7431U at United. I had paid a visit to Federal Express at the Memphis hub in June 1977 and observed part of the overnight cargo sorting. In view was a significant amount of 727 ground servicing equipment which I believe had been acquired from Eastern Airlines, once a major operator of 727QC freighters. Though public Law 95-163, essentially deregulating air cargo, would only be passed on November 9, 1977, such was the confidence this was going to occur on the part of Fred Smith, Federal's founder, that I was able to observe this equipment already in place in its Memphis hub about five months prior to the legislation's passage.

Opposite below: Air cargo on a considerably greater scale than what we just saw at Hobby on October 25 was visible at IAH on October 28, 1979, in the form of this Air France 747 freighter ready to swallow its outbound cargo.

SKY TRAVEL
N111FE
FEDERAL EXPRESS

AIR FRANCE cargo
F-BPVR

Above: Here is a pair of National Airlines' DC-10s arriving to participate in one of the connecting complexes at IAH on November 23, 1979. National is still independent but will not be for much longer.

Opposite above: This TWA 707-331B, N28727, arrived in the carrier's fleet in 1968. It was leased to Aramco (then the Arabian American Oil Company) and used to transport that company's employees traveling between Houston and Saudi Arabia. The aircraft was configured in a very low-density seating arrangement. TWA had a strong connection with the Kingdom of Saudi Arabia that began with providing technical and management support to Saudi Arabian Airlines beginning in 1946. This photo also illustrates the difficulty with having the "Trans World" titles in what was originally known as the "outline" paint scheme. This was rectified, eventually, by making the letters solid red.

Opposite below: "Commuter" carrier operations were increasing by November 11, 1979, at IAH. In addition to Metro's intra-region service seen previously, here is Rio Airways' Beech 99, N16RA.

TWA
N526MA

Rio
N924MA

Above: N3606 was previously N472US at Northwest and apparently had a bare-metal belly paint job when National acquired it in August 1979. Upon putting it into service, they elected to change the livery only where there was paint previously. Here it is at IAH on Christmas Eve 1979.

Opposite above: One of Braniff's "Ultra" color schemes was applied to only a single aircraft. Here is the sole application of "Sparkling Burgundy" on N404BN, also at IAH on December 24, 1979. Cheers!

Opposite below: Finally, here is a study in shades of orange and yellow/gold, on Air Jamaica's DC-9-30, 6Y-JGA, and National's 727-35, N4610, at Houston Intercontinental on December 30, 1979.

Braniff
N404BN

airJamaica
NATIONAL